DETROIT PUBLIC LIBRARY

W9-CCI-715

CHANEY BRANCH LIBRARY
16101 GRAND RIVER
DETROIT, MI 48227

FEB - 2007

CY

COUNT
BASIE

——— ❧ ———

COUNT BASIE

Bud Kliment

Senior Consulting Editor
Nathan Irvin Huggins
Director
W.E.B. Du Bois Institute for Afro-American Research
Harvard University

CHELSEA HOUSE PUBLISHERS
Philadelphia

Chelsea House Publishers
Editor-in-Chief Remmel Nunn
Managing Editor Karyn Gullen Browne
Picture Editor Adrian G. Allen
Art Director Maria Epes
Assistant Art Director Howard Brotman
Manufacturing Director Gerald Levine
Systems Manager Lindsey Ottman
Production Manager Joseph Romano
Production Coordinator Marie Claire Cebrián

Black Americans of Achievement
Senior Editor Richard Rennert

Staff for COUNT BASIE
Editorial Assistant Michele Berezansky
Designer Diana Blume
Picture Researcher Lisa Kirchner
Cover Illustration Alan Nahigian

Copyright © 1992 by Chelsea House Publishers, a subsidiary of
Haights Cross Communications. All rights reserved. Printed
and bound in the United States of America.

7 9 8 6

Library of Congress Cataloging-in-Publication Data
Kliment, Bud
Count Basie: bandleader and composer/by Bud Kliment
    p. cm.—(Black Americans of achievement)
    Includes bibliographical references and index.
Summary: Examines the life and career of the famous 20th-century jazz
musician.
ISBN 0-7910-1118-6.
        0-7910-1144-5 (pbk.)
1. Basie, Count, 1904–84 —Juvenile literature. 2. Jazz
musicians—United States—Biography—Juvenile literature. 3.
Afro-American musicians—Biography—Juvenile literature. [1. Basie,
Count, 1904—84 . 2. Musicians. 3. Afro-Americans—Biography.]
I. Title. II. Series.
ML3930.B33K6 1992   91-25778
781.65'092—dc20   CIP
[B]   AC MN

Frontispiece: *Count Basie performs
at the Municipal Auditorium in
Kansas City in 1939.*

CONTENTS

BLACK AMERICANS OF ACHIEVEMENT

HENRY AARON
baseball great

KAREEM ABDUL-JABBAR
basketball great

MUHAMMAD ALI
heavyweight champion

RICHARD ALLEN
*religious leader and
social activist*

MAYA ANGELOU
author

LOUIS ARMSTRONG
musician

ARTHUR ASHE
tennis great

JOSEPHINE BAKER
entertainer

JAMES BALDWIN
author

BENJAMIN BANNEKER
scientist and mathematician

AMIRI BARAKA
poet and playwright

COUNT BASIE
bandleader and composer

ROMARE BEARDEN
artist

JAMES BECKWOURTH
frontiersman

MARY MCLEOD BETHUNE
educator

GEORGE WASHINGTON
CARVER
botanist

CHARLES CHESNUTT
author

BILL COSBY
entertainer

PAUL CUFFE
merchant and abolitionist

MILES DAVIS
musician

FATHER DIVINE
religious leader

FREDERICK DOUGLASS
abolitionist editor

CHARLES DREW
physician

W. E. B. DU BOIS
scholar and activist

PAUL LAURENCE DUNBAR
poet

DUKE ELLINGTON
bandleader and composer

RALPH ELLISON
author

JULIUS ERVING
basketball great

LOUIS FARRAKHAN
political activist

ELLA FITZGERALD
singer

MARCUS GARVEY
black nationalist leader

JOSH GIBSON
baseball great

WHOOPI GOLDBERG
entertainer

ALEX HALEY
author

PRINCE HALL
social reformer

JIMI HENDRIX
musician

MATTHEW HENSON
explorer

BILLIE HOLIDAY
singer

LENA HORNE
entertainer

WHITNEY HOUSTON
singer and actress

LANGSTON HUGHES
poet

ZORA NEALE HURSTON
author

JESSE JACKSON
civil-rights leader and politician

MICHAEL JACKSON
entertainer

JACK JOHNSON
heavyweight champion

MAGIC JOHNSON
basketball great

SCOTT JOPLIN
composer

BARBARA JORDAN
politician

MICHAEL JORDAN
basketball great

CORETTA SCOTT KING
civil-rights leader

MARTIN LUTHER KING, JR.
civil-rights leader

LEWIS LATIMER
scientist

SPIKE LEE
filmmaker

CARL LEWIS
champion athlete

JOE LOUIS
heavyweight champion

RONALD MCNAIR
astronaut

MALCOLM X
militant black leader

BOB MARLEY
musician

THURGOOD MARSHALL
Supreme Court justice

TONI MORRISON
author

ELIJAH MUHAMMAD
religious leader

EDDIE MURPHY
entertainer

JESSE OWENS
champion athlete

SATCHEL PAIGE
baseball great

CHARLIE PARKER
musician

ROSA PARKS
civil-rights leader

COLIN POWELL
military leader

PAUL ROBESON
singer and actor

JACKIE ROBINSON
baseball great

DIANA ROSS
entertainer

WILL SMITH
actor

CLARENCE THOMAS
Supreme Court justice

SOJOURNER TRUTH
antislavery activist

HARRIET TUBMAN
antislavery activist

NAT TURNER
slave revolt leader

DENMARK VESEY
slave revolt leader

ALICE WALKER
author

MADAM C. J. WALKER
entrepreneur

BOOKER T. WASHINGTON
educator

DENZEL WASHINGTON
actor

OPRAH WINFREY
entertainer

TIGER WOODS
golf star

RICHARD WRIGHT
author

ON
ACHIEVEMENT

Coretta Scott King

BㄹEFORE YOU BEGIN this book, I hope you will ask yourself what the word *excellence* means to you. I think that it's a question we should all ask, and keep asking as we grow older and change. Because the truest answer to it should never change. When you think of excellence, perhaps you think of success at work; or of becoming wealthy; or meeting the right person, getting married, and having a good family life.

Those important goals are worth striving for, but there is a better way to look at excellence. As Martin Luther King, Jr., said in one of his last sermons, "I want you to be first in love. I want you to be first in moral excellence. I want you to be first in generosity. If you want to be important, wonderful. If you want to be great, wonderful. But recognize that he who is greatest among you shall be your servant."

My husband, Martin Luther King, Jr., knew that the true meaning of achievement is service. When I met him, in 1952, he was already ordained as a Baptist preacher and was working toward a doctoral degree at Boston University. I was studying at the New England Conservatory and dreamed of accomplishments in music. We married a year later, and after I graduated the following year we moved to Montgomery, Alabama. We didn't know it then, but our notions of achievement were about to undergo a dramatic change.

You may have read or heard about what happened next. What began with the boycott of a local bus line grew into a national movement, and by the time he was assassinated in 1968 my husband had fashioned a black movement powerful enough to shatter forever the practice of racial segregation. What you may not have read about is where he got his method for resisting injustice without compromising his religious beliefs.

He adopted the strategy of nonviolence from a man of a different race, who lived in a different country, and even practiced a different religion. The man was Mahatma Gandhi, the great leader of India, who devoted his life to serving humanity in the spirit of love and nonviolence. It was in these principles that Martin discovered his method for social reform. More than anything else, those two principles were the key to his achievements.

This book is about black Americans who served society through the excellence of their achievements. It forms a part of the rich history of black men and women in America—a history of stunning accomplishments in every field of human endeavor, from literature and art to science, industry, education, diplomacy, athletics, jurisprudence, even polar exploration.

Not all of the people in this history had the same ideals, but I think you will find something that all of them had in common. Like Martin Luther King, Jr., they all decided to become "drum majors" and serve humanity. In that principle—whether it was expressed in books, inventions, or song—they found something outside themselves to use as a goal and a guide. Something that showed them a way to serve others, instead of only living for themselves.

Reading the stories of these courageous men and women not only helps us discover the principles that we will use to guide our own lives but also teaches us about our black heritage and about America itself. It is crucial for us to know the heroes and heroines of our history and to realize that the price we paid in our struggle for equality in America was dear. But we must also understand that we have gotten as far as we have partly because America's democratic system and ideals made it possible.

We are still struggling with racism and prejudice. But the great men and women in this series are a tribute to the spirit of our democratic ideals and the system in which they have flourished. And that makes their stories special and worth knowing. ❧

1

A CHANCE AUDITION

JOHN HAMMOND BRACED himself against the cold as he stood in the doorway of Chicago's Congress Hotel on a November night in 1935. The 25-year-old music impresario had come from the hotel's ballroom, where he had been listening to clarinetist Benny Goodman's big jazz band. The son of a wealthy New York family, Hammond was extremely knowledgeable and enthusiastic about music and at his young age had already established himself as a critic and producer. He had also befriended many jazz musicians and frequently gave them advice and support. He had traveled to Chicago, in fact, to visit his friend Goodman as the bandleader began an important engagement at the Congress, one of the city's most prestigious night spots.

The band had played so well that during intermission Hammond had gone up to the bandleader to offer his congratulations. It had grown late in the evening, however. Hammond was ready to leave the hotel and get some sleep.

As he stepped onto the sidewalk and the lively sounds of jazz faded behind him, Hammond's

Leader of the jazz world's top swing orchestra for nearly half a century, William ("Count") Basie was also the most important musician in the group. His stripped-down piano playing set the pace for each song, and the entire band, from the bass and drums to the horns, followed in unison.

thoughts turned immediately to the blustery cold. No wonder Chicago was called the Windy City, he said to himself as he dug his chin into the top of his coat and pulled his arms close to his body. Fortunately, he had parked his Hudson automobile just across the street from the hotel and was able to get into it quickly.

Rubbing his hands and blowing on them, Hammond slid hastily across the front seat, where a bulky radio took up much of the space. Affectionately nicknamed the Golden Throat, it was an oversized shortwave receiver equipped with 12 tubes and a large speaker and was unlike any other car radio of that era. "I spent so much time on the road," Hammond said later, "that I wanted a superior instrument to keep me in touch with music around the country." Instinctively, even before he had settled in his seat, he switched it on.

Because of the late hour, few programs were being broadcast. Hammond spun the radio's dial in earnest, searching for some kind of music. Suddenly, near the high end of the dial, at 1550 kilocycles, the sound of a jazz band broke through the static. As Hammond tuned in the station more clearly, the music seized his attention. What was this? he thought, sitting up straight in his seat and leaning closer to the speaker. He continued to listen, and as he did his heart raced a little and a smile crossed his face.

What he heard was not a large band—eight or nine instruments at most, although the way they played together was remarkable. Different players came forward with impeccable timing, taking solos that sparkled but never overtook the group or slowed it down. An experienced listener with an exceptional ear, Hammond had never heard such a rhythm section before. The band's bass, drums, and piano generated a seamless beat, subtle and relaxed but also unfailingly versatile.

After listening for several minutes, Hammond felt wide awake, revived by the band's lively sound. He also stopped thinking about the cold. The air around him may have been freezing, but the music on his radio was most definitely hot.

When the song ended, an announcer said, "That was Count Basie and His Barons of Rhythm live from the Reno Club here in Kansas City. We'll be back in a few minutes." Hammond fell back in his seat and recalled the time he had heard Count Basie play piano a few years earlier in New York. He had no idea that Basie was now leading a band of his own. Then Hammond realized: If he had not heard of Basie's new group, chances were that not many other people in the music business knew about it, either.

As a pianist, Basie developed a simple playing style that allowed him to embellish and punctuate a band's sound rather than dominate it. "Basie don't play nothing," observed one musician, "but it sure sounds good."

Stunned but excited, Hammond began to think anxiously about the future. If there was one thing he liked more than discovering new music, it was telling everyone about it. As he switched on the car's ignition and pulled away from the curb into the dark Chicago night, he began to formulate a plan that would enable all of America to enjoy the Count Basie band.

At that moment in Kansas City, it was between sets at the Reno Club, and William Basie and his musicians were enjoying a break. As the bandleader, who had given himself the nickname Count, left his seat at the piano to make his way through the crowd, he considered the festive atmosphere his band's music had helped create. Full of smiles and laughter, everyone in the club seemed to be having a good time: another happy night at the Reno. For him and his band, Basie thought, the club was a good home.

Kansas City during the 1930s was crowded with places where people gathered to hear live music, and many believed that the Reno Club, a long, narrow brick building on Twelfth Street between Cherry and Locust streets, was among the city's liveliest and most entertaining night spots. Hour-long stage shows featuring local performers were held there four times a night, every night. Between shows the house band played music for the customers to dance to, and inexpensive food and alcohol were served.

Like many of the other Kansas City nightclubs, the Reno was patronized by blacks and whites but was not integrated. Each race had its own dance floor, bar, and tables. Despite the segregated facilities, the atmosphere in the club was relaxed and lively, and there was usually a friendly rapport between the performers and the customers.

Clubs such as the Reno provided terrific opportunities for musicians to earn money while having fun. Basie's band, for instance, appeared in two dif-

ferent shows: a stage performance and a set for the dancers. The group played continuously every night from about 9:00 P.M. until 5:00 A.M., taking a 10-minute break every hour. On the average, each band member earned about $18 a week plus tips; Basie, as the group's leader, took home about $21. It seemed, however, that they cared as much about making music as they did about making money.

Like most of the hundreds of musicians who lived and worked in Kansas City, Basie and his musicians loved to play. Often at the Reno—and at many of the other local nightclubs—the band members kept on playing hours after the customers had gone home. Musicians from other bands would drop by to participate in the freely improvised performances known

Music producer and promoter John Hammond (right) works with the Count Basie Orchestra at a recording session in 1940. Although Hammond nurtured Billie Holiday, Bob Dylan, Bruce Springsteen, and many other important musical talents, he called Basie "my happiest discovery."

as jam sessions or in cutting contests, extended jam sessions in which individual musicians tried to out-play one another by trading songs and solos, sometimes for hours. Everyone enjoyed the constant practice and competition, for they knew it made them superior musicians.

In addition to being a place where they could play regularly, the Reno Club offered Basie and his musicians the advantage of a long-distance radio hookup. Once a week, usually on Sundays, a microphone and transmitter were brought into the club to broadcast the band's performance to neighboring parts of the country. Basie and the other musicians did not pay much attention to the transmitter, but they knew it was a way of spreading their reputation and letting others hear how they sounded. Most likely, they figured, the radio hookup helped advertise the Reno and bring in more customers.

Yes, the Reno was a good home, Basie thought, until his daydreaming was interrupted by the radio sound man, who called the bandleader's name and gave him a signal. The break was over; it was time for the band to begin another set.

As Basie headed to the piano, he noticed people in the crowd choosing dance partners. He liked to play for dancers. He believed that they responded to his band's beat by generating one of their own, which resulted in a rhythmic give-and-take that inspired his musicians and made them play even better.

Taking his position at the keyboard, Basie watched some of his band members ascend the steps that led onto the small Reno bandstand. On the first level, the bassist Walter Page crowded close to Basie's piano and raised his bulky instrument upright, carefully inserting its neck into the small hole that had been cut out of the bandshell ceiling to make more room. On the top level, Jo Jones, the drummer, squared himself behind his drum kit. Below him, the horn players picked up their shiny brass instruments; trumpeter Oran Page and tenor saxophonist Lester Young finished a conversation and took their place with the other horn men standing in a line. Short and stout, Jimmy Rushing, the band's vocalist on certain numbers, lingered by the sidelines and waited his turn, joking with Basie and the others.

As all eight members of the band readied themselves, Basie considered their faces. He had known some of these men for years. They had eaten and traveled together, sharing rooms and good times—and hardship, too—all for the chance to create music. Such common experiences, Basie thought, had bound them closer, not only as musicians, but as people. They had become like a band of brothers who had settled in a musical community and had made a name for themselves.

Quietly, with the nod of his head and the tinkling of a few piano keys, Basie set the Rhythm Barons in motion as if he had flipped a switch. Page's bass joined the beat established by Basie's piano; Jones began to keep time on his drums. The rhythm was picked up by the horns, which started to play crisp, staccato phrases in unison. Soon, Young stepped forward, raised his saxophone (on an angle, because the bandstand was so crowded), and blew a pretty solo that drew applause. Then he stepped back as the sound of the full band surged forward and another soloist took his turn, until the tune curled around and soared, with the reed instruments calling out and the brass responding. It was a musical message, a souvenir of Kansas City jazz, and it traveled over the airwaves and into John Hammond's car.

More than 500 miles away, Count Basie sat on the bandstand, unaware that someone was busy making plans to change his life. ❧

2

THE KID FROM RED BANK

❧

WILLIAM BASIE WAS born on August 21, 1904, in Red Bank, New Jersey. Bill was Harvey Lee and Lilly Ann Basie's second son. He was raised as an only child, however, because his brother, Leroy, died while quite young.

Both Harvey and Lilly Ann Basie came from Virginia, where they had met and married before moving north to New Jersey. Harvey worked as a groundskeeper for several large estates in the Red Bank area. Lilly Ann did washing and ironing for well-to-do families that lived nearby. Although Bill's parents did not earn much money—his father took home about $40 a month, while his mother earned 50 cents for every load of laundry she washed and ironed—they made enough to buy a small house on Mechanic Street and enjoy a relatively comfortable family life.

While Bill was growing up and going to school in Red Bank, he often helped his parents with their work. During the summer, he weeded the gardens and mowed the grass on grand estate lawns that seemed

The future bandleader at age 18 (second from left) with his first professional group, Harry Richardson's Sunny Kings of Syncopation, at the Hongkong Inn in Asbury Park, New Jersey. It took Basie and his boyhood friend Elmer Williams (second from right) almost a year to hook up with an Asbury Park band.

19

Basie's interest in music was encouraged at an early age by his parents, Harvey Lee (right) and Lilly Ann (opposite page). His mother was especially influential; she gave her son his first piano lessons.

to stretch on forever. In the winter, he shoveled snow from the backyard, where his mother washed the clothes; cleared ice off the clotheslines, where she hung the wet laundry to dry; and after strapping the bales of washed and ironed clothes onto his tiny sled, he made deliveries for her at the end of the day.

Seeing how hard his parents worked frustrated Bill, but it also filled him with ambition. One day, he drew a picture of an automobile and presented it to his mother. He promised her that when he was grown, he would make enough money to buy her a car and free her from having to work. "That was the first important thing I really wanted to do in life," he recalled.

The second thing he really desired was to become a musician. Bill's parents enjoyed playing musical instruments in their spare time, and they introduced him to the world of music at a very early age. Harvey Basie played the horn. Lilly Ann was accomplished enough as a pianist to accompany the services at the church they attended.

After his mother began taking him to local dances featuring live bands, Bill yearned to play an instrument. At first he tried to play the drums. Using whatever props were available—sticks, spoons, or if neither of those was around, his hands—he pounded out rhythms on assorted objects around the house. Eventually, his father bought him an inexpensive

Scott Joplin (above) and Tom Turpin (opposite page) were two of the composers responsible for popularizing ragtime music in the early 20th century. The first black art form to gain a national audience, ragtime was the music that Basie heard most often during his youth and greatly influenced his playing style.

drum kit. Bill kept on practicing until he had mastered the instrument well enough to play in public.

It was around this time that Bill heard about Sonny Greer, a young drummer who lived in nearby Long Branch. Bill abandoned his dream of becoming a professional drummer the first time he heard Greer play. "He was just too good, too good," Bill said years later. "Everybody knew he was the champ." Greer was so good, in fact, that in 1919 he hooked up with another pianist, Edward ("Duke") Ellington, and went on to enjoy a long and distinguished career as drummer for the Duke Ellington Orchestra.

Rather than remain discouraged by Greer's expert drumming, Bill turned his attention to the piano that stood in the front parlor of his house. His mother taught him what piano-playing skills she could, then hired a German woman to give Bill additional training. For 25 cents a lesson, the teacher taught him short and easy classical pieces and fundamental finger exercises. Bill proved to be a fast learner, taking to the keyboard naturally. "I could pick out just about any song I heard," he remembered. And what he heard and played most often in his youth was ragtime.

Featuring the syncopated rhythms of West African music, ragtime was the first art form developed by black Americans to attain national prominence. Composers Scott Joplin and Tom Turpin were among those who helped bring it to the public's attention in the late 1890s. They initially wrote ragtime pieces for the piano because it was the most popular instrument in America. By the time Bill took up the piano, however, ragtime compositions were being adapted for small ensembles and contributing to the growth of an entirely new form of music: jazz.

As Bill quickly found out, ragtime piano pieces were more difficult to master than standard compositions because he had to play the lively ragtime melody with the right hand while establishing a steady marching beat with the left hand. (Combining the melody with the marching beat created the sense of "ragged time" that gave the music its name.) Nevertheless, these pieces stimulated and challenged the young musician and provided the foundation for his piano technique. "I thought a little ragtime was all you needed," he said.

When he was not practicing the piano, Bill knew plenty of other ways to have fun. From a very early age, he was attracted to all forms of show business. In particular, he loved the carnivals that set up periodically on the large vacant lot down the street from his house. As soon as a carnival arrived in town, Bill would head for the lot and offer to help. Entranced by the sights, sounds, and colors, he spent countless hours gazing at the animals, acrobats, and clowns. By the end of the carnival's run, as the circus tents were being dismantled, Bill would dream of leaving with the performers and spending his life on the road, traveling from town to town.

Besides enjoying the noisy excitement of the carnivals, Bill also loved the movies. He was friends with the manager of the Palace, a theater in Red Bank that featured films and vaudeville acts. In exchange for admission to the movies, Bill swept the theater's floors, operated its spotlights, and even turned the crank on the movie projector, just so he could watch a film again and again.

Movies in those days did not have any sound. They contained captions to convey the dialogue and advance the plot, and musical accompaniment was provided by a pianist who sat in the theater and played a score composed especially for the film. One afternoon, when the regular piano player at the Palace became ill, Bill volunteered to serve as a substitute. After all, Bill reasoned with the manager, he had already watched the film many times and

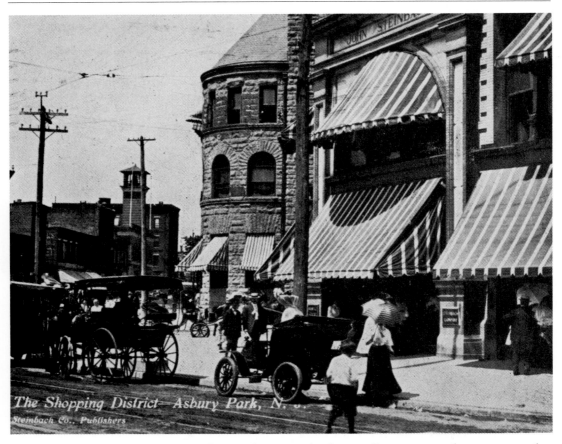

The Shopping District—Asbury Park, N. J.
Steinbach Co., Publishers

In the fall of 1923, Basie left his native Red Bank, New Jersey, for nearby Asbury Park (above and opposite page), where he began to look for work as a musician. He did not land a job there until the following summer, then lost it a couple of months later to a more experienced pianist.

knew the score by heart. Seeing no other option, the manager relented, and the screening went on as scheduled. Bill performed well enough to be invited back to accompany the evening show.

A short time later, Bill asked the theater manager for another chance to perform—not as an accompanist but as a band member in a vaudeville show. To Bill's delight, the manager granted him permission to perform on the Palace stage. As quickly as he could, the young pianist organized four of his friends—a singer, a violinist, a saxophone player, and drummer Sonny Greer—into an ensemble that the manager inserted into the lineup of acts scheduled to appear at the theater that weekend.

Bill's quintet performed for an audience consist-
ing largely of family members and friends. They
played a handful of popular songs, which were greeted
warmly by loud applause. Afterward, no one was more
pleased than young Bill. "That was really my introduction to show business," he said later. "And it was
just wonderful."

As time went on, Bill continued to play music
with local musicians at private parties, dances, and
clubs in the area. Barely a teenager, he was not
supposed to be admitted to some of these events
because he was under age. Nevertheless, he would
sneak inside with the older musicians, sometimes by
offering to carry their instruments. When he started

to play, however, he sounded experienced and no one questioned his youth—not even those times when he appeared onstage wearing short pants.

Bill's continuing musical education had an unfortunate effect on his other studies, diminishing what little enthusiasm he had for school. He enjoyed playing in the school band and winning a spot on the baseball team, but he was never a very good student. Easily distracted in class, he received poor marks and was once held back from advancing to the next grade. When he finally finished junior high school in 1923, most everyone his age had already graduated.

Tired of going to class, Bill decided not to continue on to high school. He made up his mind to work as a musician and live on his own. He later remarked that quitting school was "the worse mistake I ever made." But as a teenager filled with ambition, confidence, and show business dreams, he was sure he was making the right choice. "I don't remember that there was ever any question of me doing anything but playing music," he said. "The only question for me was where I was going to play next."

That autumn, with a friend, Elmer Williams, who played saxophone, Bill traveled to Asbury Park, a resort town south of Red Bank. Many of the local musicians found work there, but when the two teenagers arrived, they found only disappointment. Located along the shore, Asbury Park prospered in the summer but was quiet the rest of year, when there were few vacationers. Unfortunately for Bill and Elmer, the off-season had already begun by the time they arrived.

It was not until the following summer, after spending another winter in Red Bank, that Bill and Elmer could finally call themselves Asbury Park musicians. Joining Harry Richardson's Sunny Kings of Syncopation, a band that performed nightly at the Hongkong Inn, a Chinese restaurant and roadhouse, they earned about three dollars a night. Midway through the summer, Bill lost his job to a more experienced piano player and wound up parking cars in the restaurant's lot.

As the end of the 1924 summer season approached, Bill and Elmer got a few gigs at some of the local clubs. Yet success and steady employment eluded them; Asbury Park seemed to be a dead end. The boys, however, remained determined. "We had left home and school and Red Bank for good," Bill remembered. "We were musicians, and we didn't ever think about making a living doing anything except playing."

In their persistence, the two young musicians made an important contact. Earlier that summer, they had befriended a chef named Smitty who was spending the season working as a cook at one of Asbury Park's large resort hotels. Smitty hailed from Harlem, the New York City district that boasted the largest black population in the nation, and he often delighted the boys with stories of his exciting neighborhood and the musicians who lived and worked there. Again and again he encouraged them to investigate the music scene that was flourishing in uptown Manhattan's black community. Finally, at the end of the summer, after seeing how earnest the boys were about pursuing a music career, Smitty made them an offer: If they wanted to look for work in New York, they could stay at his apartment for free. Bill and Elmer accepted immediately.

And so, as autumn's quiet started to settle on Asbury Park, Bill Basie and Elmer Williams packed their belongings, pooled their money, and bought railroad tickets for their trip north. Aspirations undiminished, they were going to Harlem. ✺

3

"WITHOUT MISSING A BEAT"

◑

Basie in his mid-twenties, shortly before he began to call himself Count. "I was just a kinda honky-tonk piano player," he later said of his early years as a professional musician.

Wнен BILL BASIE and Elmer Williams arrived in New York City in the fall of 1924, the streets of Harlem unfurled before them like the grandest carnival of all, filled with lights, activity, and people. Their friend Smitty had promised them the chance to hear and make music, and as the city bustled around them, they knew that their opportunity would soon come.

Basie, in fact, decided to demonstrate his musical talent the first weekend he and Williams were in the city. Returning home from a nightclub, the young men heard music emerging from a basement saloon on Lenox Avenue. Intrigued, they went into the bar and spied a small band playing. The two New Jerseyites introduced themselves to the bandleader, trombonist Lou Henry, and then Basie asked if they could join the group for a few songs. Henry agreed.

Performing in New York City for the first time, Basie was determined to impress everyone with his showmanship and skill. "I went into my little act," he recalled, "making fancy runs and throwing my hands all up in the air and flashing my fingers. And every now and then I would also stand up and look all around without missing a beat."

Everyone in the bar seemed to be impressed by Basie's flashy keyboard work, and Henry was the most impressed of all. He offered Basie and Williams the chance to join a vaudeville act he was planning to stage at theaters across the United States. Both Basie and Williams were elated at the prospect of steady work and a chance to travel. The vaudeville circuit was going strong in the mid-1920s and paid well, making it an excellent way for a musician to earn a living.

Basie (far left) and Elmer Williams (second from right) first toured as musicians by joining the variety act Katie Krippen and Her Kiddies in 1924. Led by Lou Henry (far right), the performers traveled hundreds of miles on the vaudeville circuit before disbanding one year later.

Henry had hired Basie and Williams for an act that featured his wife, whose stage name was Katie Krippen. The act was called Katie Krippen and Her Kiddies, and it was part of *Hippity Hop*, a vaudeville revue that showcased a variety of singers, musicians, dancers, and comedians. During Krippen's portion of the show, she sang and danced to popular songs of the era, with Basie and the other musicians who accompanied her all wearing tuxedos. *Hippity Hop* hit the stage several times a day in one town before moving to the next designated stop on the tour.

Krippen and the musicians, being the only blacks in the cast, regularly experienced racial discrimination as they traveled across the United States. Humbled by the segregation laws (widely known as Jim Crow laws) that called for blacks and whites to use separate facilities, Basie and the other black members of the troupe could lodge only in black hotels or rooming houses and dine only in black restaurants. Basie was disturbed by these incidents of institutionalized racism, but he was too excited about being in a music group to let it bother him much. "I just wanted to travel and have a ball," he admitted.

Basie and Williams remained part of the *Hippity Hop* cast for more than a year. During that period, they toured the country twice before returning to New York City, where the show disbanded in 1925. At that point, Basie and Williams also parted company to pursue different prospects. Williams went on to play with many prominent jazz orchestras, including those led by Fletcher Henderson, Chick Webb, and Claude Hopkins. Basie set out to explore the Harlem music scene once more.

Having spent more than a dozen months traveling across the United States, Basie felt worldly and experienced, even though he was just 20 years old. The music he played in Krippen's act had not been very complicated, yet it had sharpened his piano-playing skills immeasurably. Now filled with confidence, he was eager to make his mark on the music world.

While Basie had been maturing as a musician, jazz had been developing, too. A combination of many types of music, including brass band marches, ragtime, spirituals, and the blues, jazz most likely originated in New Orleans around the start of the 20th century. Before long, it was being played in many different areas of the country. The music evolved as it spread, with a number of musicians, particularly those in large cities such as Chicago and Kansas City, making distinct contributions to its development.

New York City was particularly important to the shaping of jazz. The city attracted all kinds of musicians because it was America's entertainment capital and the home of Broadway theaters, sheet music publishers, movie studios, and top nightclubs. Like Basie, musicians from around the country came to New York in search of work, and when they played together, they were able to hear and compare their different styles of music making. In this creative exchange, many new musical ideas were generated and advanced the boundaries of jazz.

Pianist James P. Johnson was one of the most important jazz contributors to arrive in New York. He was a classically trained composer and pianist who performed in concert halls, but he also enjoyed playing ragtime in bars and saloons. Influenced in part by traveling blues musicians from the South, Johnson learned to alter the traditional ragtime sound by playing chords (combinations of tones that blend together harmoniously), in addition to bass rhythms, with his left hand. The result, which was heard on such Johnson compositions as "Carolina Shout" and "Keep off the Grass," loosened up the formal sound of ragtime and created a new type of music, known as stride. It was far more driving and expressive than ragtime and greatly influenced Basie and other pianists who were Johnson's contemporaries, including Duke Ellington and Thomas ("Fats") Waller.

More than anyone else, Johnson helped bridge the gap between ragtime and jazz. Yet he was not the only notable piano player to reside in Harlem when Basie returned there in 1925. Willie ("the Lion") Smith, Luckey Roberts, and Beetle Henderson were among the colorfully named pianists who performed regularly in the dozens of nightclubs and speakeasies in the district. Throughout the 1920s, it was common practice for these establishments to hire musicians as a way of entertaining the customers who came principally to enjoy alcoholic beverages, which were then illegal under Prohibition laws.

In addition to these clubs, Harlem pianists played at "parlor socials"—parties thrown by tenants who tried to scrape up enough money to pay their monthly rent by charging their guests a small admission fee. "They used to charge one dollar admission," recalled Willie Smith, who performed at many rent parties, "[and served] pigs' feet, fried chicken, mashed potatoes. Next room there'd be a card game, next room a dice game—that went on all night." The tenant would pay the pianist—and the landlord—with the evening's profits.

Basie continued his music education at rent parties and speakeasies. After a while, he began to play regularly at Leroy's, a basement club that was the first Harlem cabaret to cater exclusively to black patrons. He also spent time at the Rhythm Club, which was frequented by jazz musicians who improvised with one another. "There was always somebody sitting in," he recalled. In time, he began to move in the same circle as Johnson, Smith, and the other premier Harlem musicians. But while Basie was

James P. Johnson was one of New York City's leading jazz pianists when Basie resettled in Harlem in 1925. The friendly and gracious Johnson influenced the playing style of most of the great pianists who emerged from New York in the 1920s, including Basie, Duke Ellington, and, above all, Fats Waller, who was once Johnson's pupil.

"The first time I saw Fats Waller," Basie said of the flamboyant pianist whom he befriended in 1925, "I had dropped into the old Lincoln Theatre in Harlem and heard a young fellow beating it out on the organ. From that time on, I was a daily customer, hanging onto his every note, sitting behind him all the time, fascinated by the ease with which his hands pounded the keys and manipulated the pedals."

becoming their friend, he always made it a point to listen closely to what they played so he could improve his own technique.

In clubs such as Leroy's, the pianists often staged cutting contests. "They'd last for three or four hours," said Garvin Bushell, a Harlem musician who witnessed many such battles. "One man would play two or three choruses, and the next would slide in. You got credit for how many patterns you could create within the tunes you knew, and in how many different keys you could play."

Basie participated in many cutting contests, where the heat of competition forced him to play better and learn more. Before long, he realized that his experiences in Harlem had shaped him as both a person and a musician. "I was not from Red Bank anymore," he said. "I was from New York."

Of all the musicians Basie befriended in Harlem, Fats Waller, a protégé of Johnson's, had the greatest influence on him. Basie first encountered the chubby pianist at the Lincoln Theatre, while indulging his passion for moviegoing. Waller had been hired as the film accompanist, and Basie observed that he was improvising wildly on the theater's grand Wurlitzer organ. Basie enjoyed Waller's music so much that he kept going back to the theater and sitting in the front row, right behind the organist. At last, Waller noticed Basie and asked if he knew how to play the organ. "No," Basie replied, "but I'd give my right arm to learn."

Possessing a shared interest in music, the two became fast friends. "I used to follow him around whenever he played," Basie said, "listening and learning all the time." Waller, who was just three months older than Basie, taught his sidekick how to coax sounds from the Lincoln Theatre organ and how to improvise for movies by matching the mood of the music to the images that flashed overhead on the screen. Waller also showed Basie a few musical tricks, such as breaking up piano chords into fifths and eighths and how to "worry" a musical passage by repeating a short line of notes to create dramatic tension. Basie later said of Waller, who went on to compose such popular standards as "Ain't Misbehavin'" and "Honeysuckle Rose," "He changed my style of playing."

Basie continued to work steadily in Harlem as he made new friends who helped him improve as a pianist. He also managed to land a few gigs outside the district. He accompanied trumpeter June Clark at a nightclub engagement in downtown Manhattan, and he performed with drummer Sonny Thompson in a vaudeville act that toured Pennsylvania and New York State.

Basie resumed his travels in 1926, when he joined Gonzelle White and Her Band, a headlining vaudeville act in which the performers clowned around. Gonzelle White, who sang and danced with a diamond sparkling in one of her front teeth, set the free-spirited tone by playing the saxophone, which was considered an unusual thing for a woman to do. The other musicians chipped in any way they could. The drummer liked to grab on to the drapery during the curtain calls and ride it up to the ceiling, all the while waving to the audience. Basie performed with one leg on the piano, then turned around and played with his back to the keyboard.

After Basie had been with the band for several months, White enlarged the act by adding dancing girls, stand-up comedians, and dramatic skits. The addition of these performers required the band members to move offstage into the orchestra pit. No one complained, however. The new production, renamed Gonzelle White and Her Big Jazz Jamboree, proved to be more popular than the old one and attracted the attention of the Theater Owners Booking Association (TOBA).

TOBA had formed a black vaudeville circuit that included more than 80 black-owned or black-operated theaters as far west as Kansas City. Its shows featured black casts that played to black audiences only. According to music historian Nathan W. Pearson, Jr., TOBA "was the highest form of black theater in the first part of the twentieth century and became the training ground for many musicians who filled dance hall and nightclub orchestras in later years."

The vaudeville act starring Gonzelle White that Basie joined in 1926 "didn't have any 'names' in the cast," he said, "and we didn't do much business." As a result, when the group folded in Kansas City less than two years later, he "was broke and didn't have any way to get out of town," so he took up residence there.

Performers in TOBA shows toured constantly and often faced such harsh conditions on the road they joked that the association's initials stood for "tough on black artists." Nevertheless, the black vaudeville circuit offered them many economic and artistic opportunities. Traveling on the TOBA circuit with White, Basie saw parts of the South and the Midwest for the first time.

But his greatest revelation took place while the Big Jazz Jamboree was in Tulsa, Oklahoma. Basie was staying at the Red Wing Hotel when he was awakened one morning by music that "really got to me." He jumped out of bed to find out where the music was coming from. Sticking his head out the hotel window, he saw a group of about 10 musicians performing on the back of a flatbed truck that was driving through town, seeking to promote their appearance at a dance that evening. Basie ran after the truck and learned that the band was called the Blue Devils.

Completely absorbed by the music, Basie kept walking behind the truck—"just like I used to follow the circus parade," he said. Without using sheet music or signals, each musician seemed to know instinctively how to fit in with the others. "There was such a team spirit among those guys," Basie remembered, "and it came out in the music." It was a kind of music that Basie deeply desired to learn how to play.

Later that day, Basie met several members of the Blue Devils when they visited the theater where the Big Jazz Jamboree was playing. Shortly thereafter he got a chance to sit in with the band, although it is unclear exactly when that happened. Jimmy Rushing, the Blue Devils' vocalist, said it was the day Basie first heard the band. Basie claimed it was weeks later, in Oklahoma City, where the Big Jazz Jamboree and the Blue Devils crossed paths again.

In any case, the first time he played with them, Basie's piano skills made a favorable impression on the other band members. "Man, but he played," Rushing recalled. In turn, the Blue Devils' big-band sound continued to entrance Basie. "They had their own special way of playing everything," he said. Having developed a rapport with the Blue Devils, Basie wrote down the address of the band's leader, Walter Page, before parting so he could stay in touch with his newly made friends.

Following their engagement in Oklahoma City, Basie and the rest of the Big Jazz Jamboree moved on to the Lincoln Theatre in Kansas City, the westernmost stop on the TOBA circuit. But as soon as their booking was finished, a serious problem arose. The band had no more appearances scheduled, and owing to poor management, there was not enough money to pay anyone's way back to New York. "There we were," Basie said, "with no show and no loot and no job." Without warning, he was far from home and far from help, far from those places in Harlem where he knew he could find work. He was stranded in Kansas City. ✺

4

"A HEAVENLY CITY"

FOR JAZZ LOVERS, Kansas City was a special place during much of the 1920s and 1930s. Home to many musicians who contributed significantly to the growth and development of jazz, it boasted a unique music scene that was due in part to city politics. When Bill Basie arrived there in 1927, Kansas City was being run by Tom Pendergast, who had just become boss of the ruling Democratic party (and would remain so until 1939, when he was convicted of income tax evasion). Dedicated only to making money and retaining power, Pendergast controlled the city through an intricate system of favoritism. He bought votes and influence in exchange for granting political favors, and his henchmen held key positions in every level of city government.

During the reign of the Pendergast machine, Kansas City became known as Tom's Town and was considered "wide open." Many laws were suspended, allowing all kinds of vice, including gambling and prostitution, to thrive amid this wildly permissive atmosphere. Liquor was widely available during the

The Blue Devils, led by tuba and bass player Walter Page (fourth from left), was one of the top bands in the Southwest when Basie first heard them. He joined the group in 1928, after sharpening his piano-playing skills by performing the musical accompaniment to silent films.

41

Basie (right) sits on the bandstand at Street's Blue Room, a Kansas City night spot that featured live jazz. Tom Pendergast (opposite page), the city's remarkably corrupt political boss during the 1920s and 1930s, was an unwitting contributor to the development of Kansas City–style jazz. By encouraging vice and gang rule, which turned Kansas City into "the queen of good-time cities," Pendergast made it a place where Basie and other musicians could find steady employment, even during the lean years of the Great Depression.

Prohibition era, without a single person being convicted for buying or selling it.

Because the Kansas City police were known to ignore lawbreakers, nationally wanted criminals, among them Pretty Boy Floyd and the Barker Gang, sought refuge there. By 1934, an alarming number of local law officials had criminal records of their own: Former convicts made up 10 percent of the city's police force. "If you want to see some sin," wrote the journalist Edward Morrow, "forget about Paris and go to Kansas City."

For musicians, the lawless atmosphere in Kansas City had a positive side. With liquor flowing freely during Prohibition, the city became home to hundreds of saloons and nightclubs. In the black district alone, which covered an area of 6 square blocks—bordered by Forest, Highland, Twelfth, and Eighteenth streets—there were more than 50 night spots.

Some of these clubs boasted unusual interiors. Patrons of the Novelty Club, for instance, sat on bales of hay. Another cabaret was decorated to look like a jail, with bars on the windows and waiters who wore prison uniforms. Just as many Kansas City night spots were disarmingly simple, featuring only a wooden bar, tables, a bandstand, and a dance floor. Plain or fancy, these clubs had one thing in common: live music. "It was a heavenly city," remembered pianist Mary Lou Williams, "music everywhere."

Kansas City had always been a popular stop with vaudeville shows and bands because it was centrally located: The Missouri town boasted a riverboat port and served as a main connecting point for trains heading to the east and west coasts. Nightclubs offering constant work made it an even better stopping place for a musician. There were enough gigs to go around even after word of the staggering number of clubs began to spread. "The scene was so fine," said saxophonist Buster Smith, who later worked with Basie, "that nobody wanted to leave."

Basie could not have left Kansas City after Gonzelle White's vaudeville act disbanded in the summer of 1927 even if he had wanted to. Unable to afford a train ticket back east, he had to look for work. He had caught a glimpse of the city's lively music scene two years earlier, while stopping there with *Hippity Hop*. By chance he and some other cast members had gone for a walk that led them to Eighteenth Street, in the heart of the jazz club district. "It was one of the most fantastic sights I've ever seen in my life," Basie said. "The nightclubs were all lit up and going full blast on both sides of the street for several blocks. . . . There we were, way out in the middle of nowhere . . . and wham, we were coming into a scene where the action was greater than anything I'd ever heard of."

While this memory must have flickered in Basie's mind when he realized he was stuck in Kansas City, his thoughts soon became more immediate. He was stricken with spinal meningitis, an often fatal disease that affects the membranes enveloping the spinal cord, and he was admitted to a local hospital. He remained there for four months.

Basie eventually recovered and was released, but his massive medical expenses made him desperate for work. Because he knew how to accompany a movie, he was able to secure a job as an organist at the Eblon Theater. Whenever he had trouble following the printed score that the film company provided, he improvised his own themes and matched them to the action on the screen, just as Fats Waller had taught him in Harlem. Sometimes, as a private tribute to his friend, Basie chose to play a slow, sad version of Waller's "Honeysuckle Rose" when a character in the movie died.

At times, the job became monotonous, yet it offered Basie valuable experience. Working as an accompanist enabled him to sharpen his timing and to master playing in a variety of styles and moods. After performing at the Eblon Theater for several months, he felt that he had become an accomplished musician. He could now play all forms of popular music, including ragtime and stride, and perform in every type of situation, from a raucous saloon to a crowded movie theater.

Basie's increased confidence in his abilities at the keyboard led to an important transformation. For the purposes of promoting himself in the Kansas City nightclub circuit, he began to call himself "Count" and had business cards printed up that announced,

"Beware—The Count is Here!!" In doing so, he put himself in the company of such other royally nick-named musicians as Duke Ellington and Joseph ("King") Oliver.

Another critical example of Basie's growing confidence in his talent occurred in July 1928, when he wrote to Walter Page, the Blue Devils' bandleader. A short time later, Page sent Basie a telegram inviting the 23-year-old pianist to become a full-time member of the group. The telegram specified that the Blue Devils were headed back to Oklahoma City. Overjoyed, Basie packed his bags and left Kansas City to meet them.

Jazz was just beginning to take root throughout the Southwest when Basie joined the Blue Devils. It was played primarily by territory bands, groups of musicians who became popular in a specific territory or region. Most of these bands never recorded their music and thus failed to rise to national prominence.

Andy Kirk and His Twelve Clouds of Joy, featuring Mary Lou Williams on piano (far left), was one of the top regional orchestras to play Kansas City–style jazz during the 1920s and 1930s. The music thrived especially in Kansas City because "the town was wide open for drinking, gambling, and pretty much every form of vice," Williams recalled. "We didn't have any closing hours in these spots. We could play all morning and half through the day if we wished to, and in fact we often did."

Yet they filled an important need, bringing danceable music to Colorado, Kansas, New Mexico, Oklahoma, and Texas.

Because they sometimes had to perform one show after another in locations that were a thousand miles apart, territory bands toured constantly and often had to endure poverty, bad weather, long trips on dusty roads, and other hardships. Just as often, they were welcomed as traveling troubadours by eager listeners, and so they usually enjoyed fulfilling careers.

Of the hundred or so territory bands that toured the Southwest in 1928, the Blue Devils were one of the best known (and remain one of the best remembered, despite having made only two obscure recordings). Led by Page, a University of Kansas graduate whose 250-pound frame earned him the nickname Big 'Un, the band's home base was Oklahoma City, although they played regularly throughout Texas and as far away as Illinois and Nebraska.

The Blue Devils built their reputation on live performances and became known as tough competitors in regional battles of the bands. Territory bands, like athletes, competed regularly. When one group passed through another band's territory, a concert was arranged, with each group distributing flyers that announced the show while proclaiming itself the best band in that part of the country. The shows often attracted thousands of listeners. The bands would alternate sets, with one group trying to outdo the other's energy and skill. The audience's reaction ultimately determined the winner. The Blue Devils, in their spiffy uniforms, were the victors in many such battles.

After joining the Blue Devils in Oklahoma, Basie toured with them for almost a year, traveling throughout Texas and up through Kansas, with stops in Topeka and Wichita. During that time, he learned much about the workings of a big band. He also

THE BATTLE OF THE CENTURY!

GEORGE LEE *and his Novelty Singing Orchestra*   *vs.*   WALTER PAGE *and his Famous Blue Devils*

? Can George Lee Outplay The "Blue Devils?" Can He Outsing James Rushing? **?**

Geo. Lee's Undefeated Novelty Singing Orchestra Has Never Met Defeat. — Real Entertainment — Songs — Yes Lots.

Walter Page's Blue Devils — Champions of the South. They Have Never Run From a Contest.

Sunday Night – Nov. 25 – Dancing 9 'til ?

PASEO HALL

Admission 50c   Admission 50c

observed the spirit of cooperation and interaction that could exist among a band's members. He shared the Blue Devils' hardships as well as their joys, countering the long, cold drives with the warmth of his new friends and the applause of the fans who greeted them heartily.

Management decisions, Basie discovered, were also shared. Like other territory bands, the Blue Devils operated on a commonwealth plan. Expenses and earnings were divided evenly; most decisions about the band were discussed and decided by a vote. Under this system, Basie learned that a band's members should determine their group's direction just as it took all the instruments to produce a band's music.

"It was like a wonderful family," Basie said of the Blue Devils, and he easily made lasting friendships with many of the group's excellent musicians: trombonist Eddie Durham, alto saxophonist Buster Smith, trumpeter Oran Page (half brother of bassist Walter

The annual Battle of the Century! at Kansas City's Paseo Hall—featuring the Blue Devils (right) and George Lee and his Novelty Singing Orchestra (left)—is advertised in a local newspaper. Two of the top Kansas City–style jazz bands, they were among the many groups to build their reputation by competing against one another in live performances.

Possessing a voice with astonishing carrying power, vocalist Jimmy Rushing was one of the many talented jazzmen with whom Basie teamed up when the pianist served as a member of the Blue Devils from 1928 to 1929. Rushing, along with several other Blue Devils band members, rejoined Basie in the Count's own band several years later.

Page and nicknamed Hot Lips because he was such a skilled musician), and Jimmy Rushing, the band's soulful singer. Similarly, as each band member grew to know Basie, they came to recognize his talent as a pianist. According to jazz historian Ross Russell, whenever band members stepped forward to take a solo, "they found themselves introduced, cued, sustained, and stimulated by deft little phrases that seemed to fall effortlessly from Bill Basie's fingers."

Of all the Blue Devils, the person who influenced Basie the most was the bassist and the group's leader, Walter Page. In the earliest jazz bands, a tuba generally propelled the bass section, even though the big, bulky instrument limited an ensemble's rhythm to a medium tempo because it could accent alternate beats only. By the late 1920s, the upright string bass had replaced the tuba and was able to produce a more evenly flowing tempo. With the addition of a smoother beat, jazz became livelier and more complex.

Page had previously been a tuba player, but he made the transition to the upright string bass and became a master of the instrument. Basie learned from him the rhythmic style that seemed unique to the Southwest, a pulse that was driving yet relaxed. It was a rhythm that did not intrude on the other players; instead, it established a link, like an unspoken communication, between the Blue Devils and their leader. Basie would ultimately adapt this rhythmic style to the piano.

In spite of all the knowledge and pleasure Basie got from playing with the Blue Devils, he decided in early 1929 to leave the band. Belonging to a talented jazz ensemble had only whetted his appetite for more. "After playing with those Blue Devils," he explained, "being a musician was where it was really at for me."

Throughout the Southwest, membership in territory bands was usually loose and relaxed. It was common practice for musicians to join a group and then leave, especially when another bandleader, offering higher wages or better working conditions, tried to lure them away. As a result, the lineup of a territory band, like that of a sports team, was constantly changing.

Basie, however, was not leaving the Blue Devils to join another band. He was quitting the group because "Kansas City began calling me again," he said. The memory of its music scene remained too strong. He knew it was time to move on musically and that Kansas City was the place to do it. ◆

5

KANSAS CITY KING

W HEN COUNT BASIE returned to Kansas City after leaving the Blue Devils in 1929, he resumed working at the Eblon Theater, playing the musical accompaniment to silent films. Most evenings, he finished performing by 10:30. But instead of going home, Basie headed for the clubs. By that time of night, the jam sessions—the music making he really enjoyed—were just getting under way.

Like Basie, many of the musicians in Kansas City had belonged to territory bands at one time or another. When they gravitated back to the city (particularly during the Great Depression, the economic collapse that began in October 1929 and forced many groups to break up), these players brought with them the same urge to compete that had sparked many big-band battles throughout the Southwest. The small size of most Kansas City clubs, however, prompted a more compact kind of musical showdown. The result was the jam session, in which small, random groups of musicians played together and improvised. It soon became the most common

Bandleader Bennie Moten (seated at right) examines a musical arrangement with Basie (seated at left), who joined Moten's orchestra in 1929 as an arranger and second pianist. Basie was hired for the group, even though it was already the most successful band in Kansas City, because it needed soloists who could improvise well.

forum for Kansas City players to compete and express themselves.

Jam sessions took place at many of the Kansas City clubs that featured live music. Long after most patrons went home, the musicians kept playing well into the night, with each person trying to outplay the others. "We didn't have any closing hours in these spots," recalled Mary Lou Williams. "We could play all morning and half through the day if we wished to. . . . The music was so good that I seldom got to bed before midday."

The musicians sometimes grew so absorbed in the music that they forgot about time completely. Sammy Price, another notable pianist who performed in Kansas City, recalled an evening when he left a jam session at 10:00, went home to rest, and returned to the club three hours later. "They were still playing the same song," he said.

Jam sessions were open to all talented musicians, and word of their intensity spread quickly beyond the city's borders. Traveling musicians from around the country made it a point to pass through Kansas City, eager to match their abilities against the local jazz musicians. Similarly, local players tried to outperform the visitors. According to Ross Russell, "For certain musicians, the jam session became a way of life." Performers across the state line, in Kansas, were so eager to participate in a Kansas City jam session, recalled Mary Lou Williams, that "even bass players, caught without streetcar fare, would hump their bass on their back and come running. That was how music stood in Kansas City."

The involvement of highly talented musicians made competition in jam sessions especially heated. A person joined a jam session by performing what the rest of the ensemble was playing. When an appropriate time came, the newcomer would step forward and take a solo. On many nights, when there were a number of musicians who played the same type of instrument, they would take their turn, alternating chorus after chorus, trying to play the hottest or the sweetest in their attempt to astonish the others.

Buck Clayton, who later played trumpet with Basie, said of his first night at a Kansas City jam session: "As the evening wore on, more and more trumpet players came in to blow. To me, it seemed as if they were coming from all directions. . . . They were coming from under the rug, out of the wood-work, behind doors, everywhere. I never saw so many trumpet players in my life."

Although the competition could get fierce, jam sessions were almost always good-natured affairs pro-pelled by creativity. "It was a matter of contributing something and of experimentation," said Jo Jones. "Jam sessions were our fun, our outlet."

This constant exchange of musical ideas con-tributed to the feeling of community that existed among musicians in Kansas City. More important, it led to the development of a specific jazz style that was linked to the noisy hijinks and fervor of the jam sessions.

Basie's desire to master this home-cooked music is what lured him back to Kansas City. He began his quest by immersing himself in the local scene, sometimes as a spectator, sometimes as a participant. Listening as well as performing at these jam sessions enabled him to become more adept at playing in the local style and to learn what made it special.

Kansas City jazz, Basie discovered, featured two dominant elements: riffs and the blues. Riffs are short, strongly rhythmic musical phrases played repeatedly by one or more instruments to support a shifting chord pattern. Musicians came up with riffs spon-taneously during jam sessions. A player would start a riff, then the others would join in and play it, too. Used most often as tools for jamming, riffs may have

Vocalist Joe Turner, a Kansas City native, typified the city's lively music scene during the 1920s and 1930s. While working as a bartender at the Sunset Club in the black district, he would burst into song; his magnificent voice would carry from behind the bar into the street and entice people to enter the club instead of going into one of the many other night spots.

Basie (fourth from left) as a member of the Bennie Moten Orchestra in Kansas City during the summer of 1930. The other musicians in the group—many of whom would play in Basie's own band—are (from left to right) vocalist Jimmy Rushing; saxophonist Jack Washington; clarinetist and saxophonist Woody Walder; guitarist Buster Berry; accordionist and director Bus Moten; trombonist, guitarist, and arranger Eddie Durham; drummer Willie McWashington; tuba player Vernon Page; trombonist Thamon Hayes; trumpeter Ed Lewis; saxophonist Harlan Leonard; trumpeter Booker Washington; and pianist and bandleader Bennie Moten.

originated well before the 17th century. According to composer and music historian Gunther Schuller, "The repetition of the riff corresponds exactly to the repetitive structuring of African songs and dances, especially work and play songs."

Perfect for dancers, the wave of sound that resulted from several instruments simultaneously playing the same riff was also ideal for jamming. Individual musicians could join in easily or come forward from the group and take a solo. During the course of a jam session, many riffs could be generated; they could also be played against one another in a call-and-response pattern. As familiar riffs were played repeatedly, memorized, and passed around, groups of musicians often built entire compositions out of them.

In addition to riffs, Basie learned that Kansas City jazz musicians made distinctive use of the blues, which evolved sometime after the Civil War from a variety of sources, including field hollers and work songs (which originated in Africa and were passed down by slaves in America), church hymns and spirituals. Exclusively American and born out of the black experience, the blues refers to the feeling at the heart of the music as well as to the music itself. Early blues songs were often accompanied only by a guitar, a piano, or a harmonica. The vocalists sang of everyday concerns, most often deliverance from hardship or misfortune.

When it is played instrumentally, the blues refers to a specific musical structure, usually four bars (or measures) of notes played three times. Within this basic 12-bar framework, an accompanist can play different sets of chords to make up each 4-bar phrase, while a soloist can improvise fresh melodies on top of these chord changes. Unlike vocal blues, which is often (but not exclusively) slow and sad, instrumental blues, because its structure is strictly a compositional device, can be used to generate any kind of musical mood, happy or otherwise. Despite this difference, vocal blues and instrumental blues are both marked by simplicity, honesty, and directness of expression.

The blues was especially loved in Kansas City, where the music took root after freed slaves and performers in traveling minstrel shows brought it there. Blues vocalists such as Joe Turner enjoyed immense popularity, and instrumental blues was played constantly at jam sessions. Most participating musicians knew the standard 12-bar blues form and could adapt virtually any song to it. During a long jam session, a blues song might go on for hours with endless variations.

Through their use in jam sessions, riffs and instrumental blues became identifying characteristics of Kansas City jazz and much of the music played by territory bands. It was the lively instrumental application of the blues that made the Blue Devils sound so distinct and unique to Basie when he first heard the band, and it was the style he began to master as he

An accomplished arranger and a gifted soloist on the trombone and guitar, Eddie Durham helped Basie get a job with the Bennie Moten Orchestra. Like Basie, Durham was a former member of the Blue Devils who brought a great deal of polish to Moten's group.

continued his apprenticeship as a performer in Kansas City clubs. According to Jimmy Rushing, Basie could not play the blues when he first came to Kansas City. But by the time he left the Blue Devils and was fully immersed in the city's music scene, Basie had absorbed the bluesy, regional style and was adapting it to the full-handed stride technique he had brought with him from New York.

While circulating through Kansas City, Basie began to hear about a local bandleader and pianist named Bennie Moten. Born in Kansas City in 1894, Moten had been active in music since he was a teenager and had made his first record in 1923, when only two other jazz bands had been recorded. As the 1920s progressed, the size of Moten's band kept growing, from 6 to 8 to 10 musicians, and his reputation increased steadily, until he became the best-known bandleader in Kansas City.

Moten, in fact, was one of the few Kansas City bandleaders who had a contract with a major record label. In 1928, he and his group scored a national hit with "South." As a result, his orchestra achieved greater popularity than most other territory bands and successfully toured outside the southwestern states. Nevertheless, he remained especially popular in Kansas City because he was a local figure who had gone on to greater success.

Basie went to hear the Bennie Moten Orchestra in the early summer of 1929, after it had returned to Kansas City from a tour. Basie was impressed with the musicians' professionalism and poise. Whereas the Blue Devils had sounded somewhat rough-edged, Moten's orchestra was smooth and polished. (Accordingly, some people called him the Duke Ellington of the West, after the debonair East Coast bandleader.) Basie longed to become a band member, but Moten himself was the group's pianist, making such a wish improbable.

Basie noticed, however, that Eddie Durham, a former member of the Blue Devils, was now in Moten's orchestra, and he decided to approach him. As the two men renewed their friendship, Basie learned that Durham, besides playing trombone and guitar with Moten, was the orchestra's arranger; he adapted various pieces of music for the group and assigned parts to the musicians. Basie made several suggestions about improving the orchestra's sound, which Durham passed on to Moten. Impressed by Basie's comments, Moten invited him to join the orchestra and assist Durham with the group's musical direction. Basie accepted, thus beginning an association with the Bennie Moten Orchestra that would last almost six years.

Moten was not a dazzling pianist, but he was a shrewd and ambitious bandleader. He understood that to stay successful he had to be innovative and keep his band filled with capable musicians, many of whom could be found in Kansas City. Moten had a terrific ear for talent, and Basie did not escape his detection. In addition to hearing Basie's contributions to the arrangements and recognizing his potential as a musical thinker, Moten realized quickly that the newcomer was a talented performer.

When Basie first joined the group, he alternated piano duties with Moten during a performance. Sometimes each man played opposite ends of the same piano: Moten handled the lower section of the keyboard and tackled the bass parts; Basie sat at the upper section and took the treble parts. On other occasions, two pianos were placed back-to-back on a bandstand, allowing the two men to play simultaneously. "That was such a wonderful learning experience for me," Basie said, "because it put me so close to Bennie himself and the way he handled the band from the piano." It was, he added, "one of the most important experiences a future bandleader could have had." Eventually, though, Moten was featured at either end of the show and spent the rest of the performance conducting the orchestra or mingling with the audience, while Basie did most of the piano playing.

Basie toured frequently with the Bennie Moten Orchestra. They performed in and around Kansas City and the Southwest, then traveled to Chicago, New York, and other locations up and down the East Coast. On one of these tours, Basie made his first record, "Rumba Negro," which was part of an October 23, 1929, recording session in Chicago that produced 10 songs in all. Many other recordings followed. Of the 77 songs the Bennie Moten Orchestra recorded for the Victor Record Company, more than half featured Basie. Perhaps as a tribute to his increased role in the group, they recorded "The Count" during a 1930 Kansas City session.

Basie's role had grown larger because he had begun to assert his musical ideas more often. When he was not concentrating on his solos and accompaniments, he was thinking about how various parts would sound if other instruments played them. Basie continued to work with Durham in shaping these ideas; in their collaborations, they tried to give the Bennie Moten Orchestra a richer, more complex sound.

Their efforts were aided by Moten's practice of hiring better musicians. Constantly adjusting the orchestra's lineup, he turned most often to the Blue Devils, which was his favorite source of talent because its members had a shining reputation. They were also ripe for Moten's "raiding." During the Great Depression, the Blue Devils kept falling on hard times. Moten was able to lure many of them away by offering a steady salary and a chance at national success. Jimmy Rushing joined Moten in 1930, and soon after so did Hot Lips Page. By the winter of 1931, even

Walter Page, the band's nominal leader, had left the Blue Devils to join Moten's orchestra.

Although Moten was able to attract musicians with the promise of financial security, his own group was not immune to the hard realities of the depression. As bookings for the orchestra were cut back, it began to tour less often because venturing out on the road could be risky. "We'd come into a town and play a great gig and then we wouldn't know where the hell we were going next," Basie recalled. "We'd have to stay there until Bennie and the [promoter] came up with another arrangement somewhere. Then we would pack up and roll again."

The band members were broke, hungry, and between shows on one of these precarious tours when

During his tenure with the Bennie Moten Orchestra, Basie (back row, far right) completed his Kansas City apprenticeship. He learned the Southwest style so well, in fact, that one musician later said, "If you hear Basie, you hear Kansas City."

they assembled for a recording session at a Camden, New Jersey, studio on December 13, 1932. Despite their empty pockets and unfilled stomachs, the musicians played with remarkable verve and fullness. Riffs and solos shot out like flares, while everyone interacted with such a nonstop tightness and authority that they seemed to be thinking as one. When the session was finished, the musicians retired to a local billiards parlor, where a friend prepared a large supper of rabbit stew, beans, and corn bread, which was served on one of the pool tables. Exhausted but exhilarated, everyone ate ravenously.

That afternoon, the Bennie Moten Orchestra had cut seven tracks: "Toby," "Blue Room," "Milenburg Joys," "Lafayette," "Prince of Wales," "New Orleans," and the anthemlike "Moten Swing." Unique in their rhythms and intensity, these songs have since become regarded as some of the finest examples of Kansas City jazz ever recorded. The session also served as early evidence of Basie's fine work with bassist Walter Page, the nucleus of the Count's later band. According to music historian Stanley Dance, "The tremendous drive he and Basie created together was the fundamental source of inspiration on the session."

As it turned out, the session in Camden marked the last time this version of the Bennie Moten Orchestra ever recorded together. Although the group was soaring musically, the depression continued to keep their fortunes in the dust. As they made their way back to Kansas City from the East Coast in 1933, business fluctuated wildly. Dissatisfied and anxious, many of Moten's musicians, including Durham, abandoned the orchestra on the way to Missouri. Some left almost as quickly as they joined.

The orchestra continued to struggle even after it reached the Southwest, a usually dependable source for work. Bookings for large groups had begun to decline. To make matters worse, other territory bands had gained in skill and popularity and were success-fully competing with the Bennie Moten Orchestra for the remaining gigs. The hard times led to frustration and disputes among Moten's band members.

The situation finally came to a head in mid-1933, when the orchestra was scheduled to begin an engagement at the Cherry Blossom Theater in Kansas City. Several of the musicians voted to break away from Moten and try to make it on their own. Much to Basie's surprise, they elected him the bandleader. Basie accepted the position, although he felt uncom-fortable about the rebellion and apologized to Moten. In any event, the group completed the booking under its new name, Count Basie and His Cherry Blossom Orchestra, and continued to be featured at the theater periodically.

In 1934, Basie's orchestra traveled to Little Rock, Arkansas, where they worked intermittently for the next several months, even though the band's mem-bership—and luck—kept shifting. Neither Basie nor his musicians had enough of a reputation in Arkansas to generate steady work, so the group gradually disintegrated. Basie was learning firsthand how bad the depression could be. "The suit pants I was wearing got so worn," he said, "that when I went down the sidewalk, I had to stay close to the wall to keep my raggedy seat out of sight."

By early 1935, Basie and some of the other musicians who had deserted Moten returned to Kansas City and rejoined their former leader, who welcomed them back with no hard feelings. Moten was even able to secure an important booking for his re-formed group: several nights at one of the leading dance spots in the West, the Rainbow Gardens in Denver, Colorado. When his band left for the engagement, however, Moten stayed behind to have a tonsillectomy; he planned to meet them on the road after having the operation on April 2.

Moten never made it to Denver. During the surgery to remove his tonsils, either the doctor's hand slipped or Moten jerked suddenly—whatever the case, the physician's scalpel severed the bandleader's jugular vein, and he bled to death. Receiving the tragic news during their rehearsals in Denver, the band members were so devastated that they could barely make it through their opening-night performance. Moten's brother Ira tried to assume leadership of the band, but the musicians, dispirited and demoralized, drifted apart after a few weeks.

Basie headed back to Kansas City, where Sol Steibold, a friend who managed the Reno Club, offered him a job as leader of the house band. By then Basie had virtually completed his Kansas City apprenticeship. "Years in hard-hitting southwestern bands had made him an exceptional accompanist," observed music historian Mark Tucker. "He now knew how to answer back when the brass and reeds shouted, how to make himself heard above the rest of the band,

By 1935, Basie was ready to form his own band. This photograph is the earliest known illustration of the entire Count Basie Orchestra, taken in 1937. The musicians are (from left to right) saxophonist Herschel Evans; trombonist and arranger Eddie Durham; trumpeter Buck Clayton; saxophonist Earl Warren; trumpeter Bobby Moore; trombonist Dan Minor; saxophonist Jack Washington; trumpeter Ed Lewis; trombonist Benny Morton; saxophonist Lester Young; drummer Jo Jones; guitarist Freddie Greene; bassist Walter Page; and Basie.

and how to blend in with the rhythm section the moment the lead instruments dropped out."

Eager for a new challenge, Basie accepted the post. At age 30, he believed he was experienced and mature enough to lead a Kansas City group. He had learned from Moten that a bandleader should be even-tempered, strong-willed, and reasonable. Just as important, he should hire highly skilled players who were extremely compatible.

Installed at the Reno Club, Basie began to assemble a team of formidable musicians who co-operated with each other. As the months wore on, he hired many of his former colleagues: Walter Page, Blue Devils alto saxophonist Buster Smith, and two musicians from the Cherry Blossom Orchestra, tenor saxophonist Lester Young and drummer Jo Jones. Jimmy Rushing and Hot Lips Page, both of whom worked at the Reno Club as solo acts, were gradually absorbed into Basie's band, like family members at a reunion. Ultimately, there were nine musicians in all:

three played rhythm instruments, three performed on brass (trumpets), and three were on reeds (saxophones). Basie called it his "three, three and three band," although the group was eventually named the Barons of Rhythm, to complement their leader's royal nickname.

As the band's lineup was strengthened, so was its sound. Count Basie and His Barons of Rhythm performed every night at the Reno Club and then jammed into the early hours of the morning. Some weeks, it was estimated, the musicians played together for more than 60 hours. Instead of wearing them out, the practice only made them better. "We felt completely relaxed and we got accustomed to playing with one another," Basie said, "and it was easy to work out on-the-spot arrangements that really jumped."

Playing and jamming constantly, Basie and his band relied heavily on riffs and blues progressions to create original compositions and adaptations of popular songs. No matter whether they were worked out during rehearsals or performances, these arrangements were not usually written down; rather, they were remembered by the musicians who played them. As a result, they were called head arrangements. Accordingly, a typical set by Basie and His Barons of Rhythm consisted mainly of "heads." "I don't think we had ever four or five sheets of music up there," Basie said of the Reno Club performances. "But we had our own things and we could always play more blues and call it something. . . . We had a ball every night."

As the band's popularity spread, a microphone and radio transmitter were brought into the Reno Club each week to broadcast the group's performances. One such broadcast in late 1935 caught the attention of John Hammond, who enjoyed the band so much that he started listening to them regularly and published enthusiastic reviews of their radio concerts. The following spring, he traveled to Kansas City to meet Basie and hear the band in person. He was not disappointed. "My first night at the Reno in May 1936 still stands out as the most exciting musical experience I can remember," Hammond said. "This Basie band seemed to have all the virtues of a small combo, with inspired soloists, complete relaxation, plus the drive and dynamics of a large orchestra."

Returning east, Hammond persuaded Willard Alexander, a representative of the Music Corporation of America, a prominent booking agency for dance bands, to make the trip to Kansas City to hear Basie and his group. Once he did, Alexander became as wildly enthusiastic as Hammond about the band's talent and potential. In the fall of 1936, he signed Count Basie and His Barons of Rhythm to an exclusive contract—the first black band his agency had ever agreed to manage. Alexander's plan was to have the musicians travel to New York, where they would perform and receive heavy promotion.

With the promise of professional management, all the pieces seemed to be in place for Basie and his men to take the legacy of the Blue Devils and the Bennie Moten Orchestra and push Kansas City jazz to new heights. But this time the entire nation would be listening. ✤

6

"JUMPIN' AT THE WOODSIDE"

BEFORE COUNT BASIE and his band left for the East Coast in the fall of 1936, several changes were made in the group's lineup. At the urging of Willard Alexander and John Hammond, who believed the orchestra should be the same commanding size as other popular big bands, Basie added a trombone section as well as another tenor saxophonist. A few personnel substitutions were also made: Hot Lips Page, who decided to leave the orchestra to pursue a solo career, was replaced by trumpeter Buck Clayton, and alto saxophonist Caughey Roberts took over for Buster Smith, who did not want to go on the road. When it finally left Kansas City on Halloween night, 1936, the enlarged band contained 13 members, plus vocalist Jimmy Rushing and Basie, and had been renamed Count Basie and His Orchestra.

Throughout his career as a bandleader, Basie possessed a personality that was as diplomatic and straightforward as his musicianship. Quiet and modest, firm yet fair, and equipped with a wry sense of humor, he was a generous father figure to dozens of musicians who joined him on the bandstand and learned and prospered under his leadership. "It's always been a family feeling," guitarist Freddie Greene observed, "from the Thirties right on."

There were a few setbacks at first. The newly added musicians were more than competent, but the enlarged group, unlike the nine original Barons of Rhythm, was not used to performing as a unit and sounded sluggish. All the musicians, old and new, had to learn how to function as an ensemble. "I wanted my 15-piece band to work together just like those nine pieces," Basie later said, ". . . to think and play the same way. I wanted those four trumpets and three trombones to bite with real guts. BUT I wanted that bite to be just as tasty and subtle as if it were the three brass I used to use." He knew, however, that it would take time for his new big band to forge their musical identity and sound as tight and driving as his old one.

Confident that the Count Basie Orchestra would improve with every opportunity to perform that the musicians received, Alexander booked the group for an extended series of appearances on their route to New York. Yet their shows continued to be marked by difficulty and disappointment. After Kansas City, the orchestra's first booking was a monthlong engagement at the Grand Terrace, a posh Chicago ballroom that featured a lavish floor show accompanied by a fancy musical score to be played by the visiting band. Disaster loomed because most of Basie's musicians could not read sheet music; they knew how to play head arrangements only.

Unable to perform the score as written, the orchestra tried to fake it. "We had to do the best we could, which was nothing," recalled Buck Clayton. "We abused that show every night we were there."

Luckily for Basie and the rest of his troupe, veteran bandleader Fletcher Henderson stopped by one of the shows. He saw how the group was struggling and offered to lend Basie his own band's arrangements for the show. With Henderson's coaching and encouragement, the Count Basie Orchestra was able to satisfy the Grand Terrace's management and clientele. "He was the only bandleader in the business who ever went out of his way to help me," Basie later said of Henderson. "Without his help, we'd have been lost."

Clearly, the orchestra's luck was turning. Prior to leaving Kansas City, Basie had made the mistake of signing a recording contract with Decca Records for very little money. The contract stipulated that the group would record exclusively with Decca for 3 years and would receive a flat rate of $750 for 24 songs; there was no provision for a royalty payment for each record sold. As a result, some of the orchestra's biggest hits in later years yielded no additional income. John Hammond, who eventually renegotiated the contract so the band members could receive a modest royalty for their work, called it "probably the most expensive blunder in Basie's history . . . typical of some of the underscale deals which record companies imposed on unsophisticated [artists]."

Motivated in part by his own frustration with Decca, Hammond arranged to record Basie and a few others secretly for another company. On Monday morning, November 9, 1936, after playing all night at the Grand Terrace, Basie and 5 of his musicians crowded into a 12-by-15-foot room and recorded 4 tracks: "Shoe Shine Boy," "Evenin'," "Boogie Woogie," and "Oh, Lady Be Good." Despite the primitive recording equipment, Hammond was able to capture the quiet fire and unique virtuosity that Basie and his musicians could create. "Each [track] was cut without interruption, each a flawless performance," Hammond said. "Packed into that small room the band was free and swinging."

The recordings were released on the Vocalion label under Jones-Smith, Inc., after drummer Jo Jones and trumpeter Carl Smith, both of whom participated in the session, rather than billed under Basie's name. All four songs remain particularly memorable because

"I am astonished they were not fired," John Hammond said of the Count Basie Orchestra's shoddy performance at Chicago's Grand Terrace in 1936. Fortunately for Basie and his musicians, bandleader Fletcher Henderson (above) "came to the rescue, allowing Basie to use half his library of arrangements."

Saxophonist Lester Young was a featured performer on the first songs ever recorded by the Count Basie Orchestra, in 1936. His ethereal music may have sounded odd at first, but jazz listeners were soon praising his unique sense of melody and rhythm, and Young was eventually recognized as one of the fathers of modern jazz, a true pioneer who altered its sound and direction.

they were the first to feature Lester Young, the tenor saxophonist considered by many to be the most innovative musician ever associated with Basie. A native of Mississippi, Young was moody and eccentric, and his playing style seemed as quirky as his personality: The light, lyrical music he coaxed from his instrument contrasted sharply with the rich, heavy tenor saxophone sound then being popularized by Coleman Hawkins and others. Young shone especially in his solo on "Oh, Lady Be Good," which is now widely held to be one of his all-time best performances.

While Basie's small group was making musical history, the full orchestra continued to struggle. After the Grand Terrace engagement and a succession of other one-night appearances, the band finally arrived in New York City, where it was scheduled to appear for a month at the Roseland Ballroom. The musicians were still not playing together properly, however, and on opening night—Christmas Eve, 1936—they showed they were not ready for their Manhattan debut. Basie had to put so much effort into trying to direct them and keep the band unified that for most of the show he had his back turned to the audience. Describing the disaster, critic George Simon wrote, "If you don't believe the band is out of tune, just listen to the reed section. If you don't believe the reed section is out of tune, just listen to the brass section. And if you don't believe that, just listen to the band!"

Some of the criticism directed at the group was probably unavoidable. Hammond, Alexander, and others had generated so much enthusiastic publicity about the Count Basie Orchestra before the group arrived in New York that it was practically impossible for the musicians to live up to the advance buildup. In addition, a few of the band members were genuinely inexperienced. They had come to New York with old instruments patched together with rubber bands, and they were unable to stay in tune. "We all had a lot to learn," Buck Clayton admitted.

Despite their initial disappointment, Basie's musicians remained undiscouraged. The same enthusiasm that had sustained so many of them through tough times in Kansas City came forward once again to help them persevere. They remained staunchly dedicated to Basie, aware that his leadership had already brought them a long way. "New York wasn't easy," Clayton said. "The band scuffled, and it starved. But it didn't seem to matter. Playing was the important thing. Sticking together and making a go of the band was our ambition. We wouldn't think of leaving Basie."

With the band members focused and unified, it was only a matter of time before their music sounded tight and harmonious. They practiced regularly at the Harlem hotel where Basie and some of his musicians had chosen to stay: the Woodside Hotel, a popular place among black athletes and show people. The rehearsals were held in the basement and typically began with Basie setting a musical phrase and tempo for the trumpet section, contrasting ones for the trombone section, and yet another musical phrase and tempo for the saxophones. Surrounded by the sounds of the different sections surging in and out, individual players challenged and complemented one another as they worked out their solos.

Following this pattern, Basie and his orchestra improved their old head arrangements while constructing new ones out of riffs, blues progressions, and fragments of other songs. Rehearsing by day and performing at night, the enlarged group was able to rebuild its collective sound, fine-tune its rhythmic snap, and create a fresh and dazzling interplay between the soloists. In fact, many of the band's practice sessions in the Woodside's basement, which adjoined the hotel's dining area, ended with the waiters and patrons dancing to the music being cooked up next door.

The band's sound at this time was further enhanced by a couple of changes in its lineup. At John Hammond's suggestion, Basie hired guitarist Freddie Greene to fill out and frame the band's rhythm section. Another significant addition, also at Hammond's urging, was singer Billie Holiday, whom Basie brought in to alternate vocals with Jimmy Rushing.

Like Basie, Holiday had been discovered by Hammond. A Baltimore native, she was a dreamy-sounding singer who was remarkably able to communicate the mood and meaning of a song. She also possessed an acute sense of timing that Hammond believed would complement perfectly the rhythms produced by Basie's orchestra. Holiday performed

One of several female vocalists to tour with the Count Basie Orchestra, Billie Holiday performs at the Meadowbrook Lounge in Cedar Grove, New Jersey, in 1937. At the end of the decade, Holiday pursued a solo career that soon elevated her to the top of the New York jazz scene.

with the band for about a year before leaving to find success as a solo singer—indeed, she is now considered to have been one of the greatest jazz vocalists of all time. During the period she sang with the Basie band, she helped bring the group a noticeable share of attention.

Holiday was part of the orchestra when it debuted in early 1937 at New York's Apollo Theater, and it proved to be one of the band's most important early engagements. Located on 125th Street in the heart of Harlem, the Apollo was the district's premier theater. Since it first opened its doors in 1934, virtually every notable jazz band appeared there.

The Apollo held a special mystique in part because of its highly critical patrons. When the performers were good, the audience voiced its approval loudly. "But if you turn them off," said Holiday, "brother, watch out! The inhabitants of the Buzzard's Roost [the top balcony] can pick your carcass clean." They would hoot and holler until the performers had left the stage, utterly shamed.

Basie and his band were justifiably nervous on March 19, the day they were scheduled to open at the theater. The assembled audience was making so much noise that Ralph Schiffman, the Apollo's owner, decided to postpone the opening acts and put Basie's band on first. As the jittery musicians gathered onstage, stood at their bandstands, and started to play, it became clear to Basie that the rehearsals and one-nighters had made a difference. His band was sounding full, in tune, and powerful. The crowd knew it, too. Throughout the performance, they kept roaring back their approval.

After the show was finished, Schiffman went backstage to congratulate Basie and found the bandleader so emotionally overwhelmed that it took several minutes for him to compose himself. In the years to come, Basie and his orchestra would play the

Apollo many times; but their first night at the theater remained special. "Nobody in Harlem will ever forget the opening," Hammond said. "Basie passed the test. He was on his way."

Buoyed by the enthusiastic response, the orchestra continued on to performances at venues in Philadelphia, Baltimore, Washington, D.C., and other cities along the East Coast, picking up steam and building its reputation as it went. Onstage, the musicians' talent and collective confidence grew to be so persuasive that they won new fans wherever they played. Individually, too, the soloists in the group became focal points for the listeners' attention.

Heavyset Jimmy Rushing, for instance, became an audience favorite because of his distinct voice and large presence. Later nicknamed Mr. Five by Five because he seemed as wide as he was tall, Rushing sang the blues in a forceful, near-tenor voice, pitched slightly higher than many other male blues singers, who sang in thick, low registers. Equally sincere and expressive, Rushing's delivery was also strangely elegant, imposing "a romantic lyricism upon the blues tradition," said author Ralph Ellison, who once described Rushing's voice as "a blue flame in the dark." Basie's horn players also delighted the listeners. Buck Clayton, for instance, played melodies so purely and gracefully on his trumpet that his sound was immediately distinguishable.

Of all the horn players, however, it was the competition between two of the tenor saxophonists, Lester Young and Herschel Evans, that attracted the most attention. The two men had completely contrasting styles: Young's tone was light and airy; Evans's sound was hearty and robust. Sitting on the bandstand at either end of the horn section, they alternated solos like duelists. Each man seemed to challenge the other, pushing him—and the entire band—to play harder. Like a Kansas City jam session

in miniature, the onstage rivalry between Young and Evans appeared so fierce and intense that some listeners believed the two men genuinely did not like each other.

Basie himself, of course, strengthened the group's appeal. A visible and appealing bandleader, he modestly refused to take long, flashy solos. "I love to play," he said, "but this idea of one man taking one chorus after another is not wise. . . . Therefore, I fed my dancers my own piano in short doses and when I came in for a solo, I did it unexpectedly, using a strong rhythm background behind me. That way, we figured, the Count's piano wasn't going to become monotonous."

Basie's piano playing may not have been the most obvious or prominent sound in the orchestra, but he

Nicknamed the All-American Rhythm Section, (from left to right) guitarist Freddie Greene, drummer Jo Jones, bassist Walter Page, and pianist Basie favored a beat that was relaxed but steady, a southwestern tradition. "Bennie Moten's band played a two-beat rhythm such as one-and-three," explained Jones. "Walter Page's band played a two-and-four. . . . When those rhythms met in the Basie band there was an even flow—one, two, three, four . . . like a bouncing ball."

clearly kept the songs moving and the group together. Like his leadership, his playing always lent the other musicians support. "Basie contributes the missing things," observed Freddie Greene. "He makes different preparations for each soloist and that way, at the end of one of his solos, he prepares an entrance for the next man. He leaves the way open."

Almost offhandedly, Basie would use a few well-chosen notes to highlight or fill gaps in the band's overall sound. The timing and placement of those notes served to boost the other players (as well as listeners). Said jazz writer Martin Williams, Basie "shifted the very function of jazz ensemble piano. He no longer accompanied in the old way: he commented, encouraged, propelled and interplayed."

In addition to their steady stream of live performances, Basie and his orchestra also began to make records. At their first Decca session, on January 21, 1937, in New York City, they recorded four tracks: the Fats Waller composition "Honeysuckle Rose"; Basie's tribute to Waller, "Pennies from Heaven"; "Swinging at the Daisy Chain"; and "Roseland Shuffle," to honor the ballroom in which they had made their dubious Manhattan debut. On these first releases, the group sounded confident and ready and played with ease and skill. Jazz critic Whitney Balliett wrote that the enlargement of Basie's band had seemed at first "as if a trim man had suddenly gained twenty-five pounds." By 1937, when they began to record, "the extra weight," he observed, "had been converted to muscle."

Under the terms of their Decca contract, Basie and his orchestra recorded regularly. (They ultimately made 57 recordings for the label: 10 piano pieces, 21 full band instrumentals, and 26 featuring vocals.) In general, the group's material included popular songs and band originals—head arrangements that had been worked out in Kansas City or New York.

Many of the original songs had stories behind their titles. "John's Idea," for instance, featured the dueling tenors of Lester Young and Herschel Evans and was dedicated to John Hammond. "Panassie Stomp" was named in honor of the French jazz critic Hugues Panassie, who had written enthusiastically about the orchestra. "Shorty George" was titled after a Harlem dance step. "Every Tub" was inspired by an expression from Basie's vaudeville days: "Every tub sits on its own bottom" (meaning that people should be responsible for themselves). One of the most enduringly popular songs recorded by the Count Basie Orchestra was "Jumpin' at the Woodside," a rollicking tribute to the hotel in which the band had mastered its music.

With each new release, the musicians became recognizable to listeners through their solos. Basie's piano style, in particular, sounded immediately distinct and completely individual. While retaining the bounce and flourish of a stride pianist, he played far fewer notes. "Every now and then, plink-plink," said pianist Eddie Heywood, describing Basie's terse style, "but it was the right plink-plink."

While some attributed Basie's stripped-down piano playing to the same modesty that kept him from taking long solos, his technique was more likely shaped by his apprenticeship in Kansas City. Musicians there, according to bassist Gene Ramey, had an expression: "Say something on your [instrument]. . . . Tell us a story and don't let it be a lie. Let it mean something, if it's only one note." As Basie developed musically, he took this sentiment to heart. He was using relatively few notes, but each one said and meant a lot.

By playing less, Basie was, in fact, changing the role of the piano in the jazz orchestra. He was using the instrument percussively rather than melodically, to heighten and assist the band's rhythm section. He

On the night of January 16, 1938, immediately after performing at New York City's Carnegie Hall, Basie led his band in a cutting contest against the Chick Webb Orchestra. "Count Basie did it!" Metronome magazine reported. "For years, nobody was able to lick Chick Webb and his Chicks within the walls of his own Savoy Ballroom, but on January 16, notables such as Duke [Ellington], [Red] Norvo, [Buster] Bailey, [Eddie] Duchin, [Gene] Krupa and [Benny] Goodman heard the Count gain a decision over the famed Chick."

was smoothing out the beat while making it pop and sparkle. At the time, such an approach was totally without precedent.

Basie's fresh sound kept his records selling briskly; each new release seemed to do better than the one preceding it. In July 1937, to supplement the band's supply of material for recording and performing, Basie hired his collaborator in the Bennie Moten Orchestra, Eddie Durham, who served as a member of the orchestra as well as its arranger for a year.

Around the time that Durham came on board, Basie's orchestra cut its breakthrough record, "One O'Clock Jump." The song, recorded on July 7, was a jaunty collection of sturdy riffs punctuated by fine solos played by Clayton, Evans, and Young. The song caught on immediately with dancers and introduced many new listeners to the strengths and style of the Basie band.

Credited to Basie (but in fact a collaboration by several band members), "One O'Clock Jump" was a head arrangement dating back to the band's Kansas City performances. As such, it proved unusually durable. A version by the Benny Goodman Orchestra was a hit all over again in 1938, when it became that group's first million-selling record; by 1940, "One O'Clock Jump" had been recorded a dozen different times. Nevertheless, it was always associated with Basie and his band—to the point that it became their theme song and was featured at nearly every one of their performances in the years to come.

By 1938, following a hit record and a year of activity that included concerts, broadcasts, and more recordings, the band's popularity had steadily increased. The year began memorably, with a pair of dramatic performances. On January 16, 1938, Basie and four of his musicians—Buck Clayton, Freddie Greene, Walter Page, and Lester Young—were invited to participate in Benny Goodman's historic concert at Carnegie Hall, one of the first times jazz was presented in the prestigious concert hall.

For their portion of the program, Basie and his colleagues joined Goodman and his band onstage for an extended jam session based on "Honeysuckle Rose." Their performance was a highlight of the show, especially for those listeners who had been unfamiliar with Basie's style and skill. On the whole, the concert was a resounding success, thrilling both the audience and the participating musicians.

For Basie and his band, however, the evening had just begun. After Goodman's concert concluded, the five musicians left the classy confines of Carnegie Hall to meet the rest of the orchestra uptown, at the Savoy Ballroom, where they were scheduled to battle the Chick Webb Orchestra. The Savoy, which occupied the entire second floor of a block-long building on Lenox Avenue between 140th and 141st streets, had opened in 1926, and it quickly became the fanciest, most popular place to dance in Harlem. Equipped with marble staircases and two bandstands that could "disappear," it was nicknamed "the home of happy feet" because it had a polished maple dance floor, measuring 10,000 square feet, that bounced slightly when it was filled with dancers.

The Savoy's patrons demanded good dance music, and Webb's group, which in January 1938 included a versatile 19-year-old vocalist named Ella Fitzgerald, served them a steady diet of swinging rhythms. Acting as the Savoy's house band, the Chick Webb Orchestra defended its turf against visiting groups in musical contests that drew large crowds and much publicity.

Knowing Webb's band was tough to beat but sure that Basie's group would offer stiff competition, thousands of jazz fans, including bandleaders Duke Ellington, Lionel Hampton, and Benny Goodman, gathered at the Savoy on the night of January 16 to witness the musical face-off. The atmosphere was charged with expectation; the two bands were ready to fight. "Off the stand everybody was real friendly and very diplomatic," recalled Beverly Peer, Webb's bassist. "But when we got up on the stand—well, everybody was going for blood!"

The bands alternated songs, and as they did, their energy level kept rising. Audience members began to wave handkerchiefs and pierce the air with shouts and stomps. When Webb, sweat dripping onto his cymbals, played a solo on the drums, his fans started to cheer. Basie struck back by running his hands up and down the keyboard like lightning.

In each group, the brass and reed sections rang out, while in front, Billie Holiday, dressed in blue, and Ella Fitzgerald, garbed in white, took turns singing—and trying to win the crowd's affection. Both bands played that way for two hours, and the intensity never let up.

When the battle was over, the results were split. The audience voted Webb's band the winner, but most of the musicians and critics in attendance claimed that the Count Basie Orchestra had been victorious. Even George Simon, the critic who had panned Basie's debut at Roseland, was convinced. His review was headlined BASIE'S BRILLIANT BAND CONQUERS CHICK'S! In any event, Basie's orchestra was invited back to the Savoy for several nights in March and May 1938 to perform as the featured band.

A few months after their uptown success, the group was booked to play at the Famous Door, a club in midtown Manhattan. It turned out to be a crucial engagement. Located on Fifty-second Street, which was lined with music clubs and nicknamed Swing Street, the Famous Door had a small, narrow interior and a stage that usually held no more than five musicians. Willard Alexander had come up with the unusual idea of putting Basie's big band into such a small space, believing that the club's cramped quarters would perfectly showcase the group's abilities. Viewers at close range, he thought, could actually see the musicians interact; observed close up, their precision would seem razor-sharp.

Besides, Alexander reasoned, if the club appeared overcrowded, the band would seem more popular. "If people couldn't get in," he said, "people would want to get in."

Opening night was July 11. By then, Basie's orchestra, which was already brimming with talent, included the master trombonist Dicky Wells and trumpeter Harry Edison (whose nickname, inspired by his playing, was Sweets). About 75 patrons crowded into the Famous Door, and 25 more surrounded its tiny bar.

Barely fitting inside the cramped quarters of the Famous Door in the summer of 1938, Basie and his musicians overwhelmed the small club with their dominating rhythm. The high-powered performances that the Count Basie Orchestra gave at this New York City night spot quickly earned the band a national reputation.

As the band members began their set, it was immediately obvious that Alexander had been correct in his thinking: The sound and presence of the musicians was overwhelming. "In that small space, fourteen men playing as one," Alexander recalled, "you could feel the pulsations inside you." The band's dominating rhythm seemed to fill every corner of the little club, while the surging brass threatened to level it. "When they let you in that door," wrote critic Ralph Gleason, "it was like jumping into the center of a whirlwind. That sound was almost frightening."

Almost immediately, the band became a national sensation. For weeks afterward, audiences lined up outside the Famous Door, eager to get inside to hear the country's hottest "new" group. Basie and his musicians did not disappoint; their performances seemed to just get better. "Those guys didn't just play together," Alexander recalled, "they used to breathe together. . . . That's what brought the crowds to the Door."

In time, a radio transmitter was brought into the club, which spread news of the band's triumph even farther. (During these broadcasts, all patrons, drinks in hand, had to step temporarily outside because the club lacked enough room for them, the radio engineers, and the equipment.) When the broadcasts began, Alexander said, "people all over the country were sitting in on the birth of a great big band."

The Count Basie Orchestra was initially scheduled to appear at the Famous Door for six weeks. Because of the tremendous response the group provoked, it was held over for three months. "That turned out to be our biggest break," Basie said. "That was the place where we really went over and stayed over." One year later, the band returned to the club that had launched it to national fame, and it appeared there for most of the summer.

Late one night during this period, the bandleader sat in his room at the Woodside Hotel and reflected on all that had happened during the past two years. He thought about how far his group had come, managing to overcome looseness and inexperience on its way to achieving popular success. Remembering how his leadership abilities had been tested and realizing that he had passed each test with flying colors, Basie said to himself, "My goodness, this was really something."

7

SWINGIN' THE BLUES

◆❦◆

BIG-BAND JAZZ was the reigning popular music in America at the time that Count Basie and His Orchestra became nationally successful. All over the country, in ballrooms, nightclubs, and theaters, as well as on record and radio, hundreds of bands played in styles ranging from sweetly romantic to dramatically rhythmic. Appealing to listeners of all ages, big-band music was especially loved by young people, who danced and socialized to its rich, full sound. Enthusiastic young fans would follow the progress of their favorite bands as though they were sports teams, memorizing the lineups, the key players, and the hits.

In concert, the most popular bands inspired powerful reactions: Crowds rushed the stage and danced in the aisles, creating scenes much like those in today's pop music world. "It was an era when a lot of popular music was good, and a lot of good music was popular," songwriter Gene Lees said. "To hear one of the bands straining the walls of some arena or theater or pavilion, without all the paraphernalia of modern amplification, was one of the great thrills in music."

The years when big-band music was at its peak of popularity, from the mid-1930s through the mid-1940s, became known as the Swing Era because of the lively sounds and rhythms that the bands produced. *Swing* refers to the point in a performance, either by a soloist or a group, when all the rhythmic

Basie possessed "an extraordinary economy of style," according to John Hammond. "With few notes he was saying all that [Fats] Waller and [Earl] Hines could say pianistically, using perfectly timed punctuation—a chord, even a single note—which could inspire a horn player to heights he had never reached before."

and melodic elements are in unison, interacting and proceeding smoothly. "When a band begins to swing," Stanley Dance observed, ". . . the feeling was much the same as when an airplane . . . suddenly took off after roaring along the runway." Swing, in fact, is really just another name for jazz; all styles of jazz, if they are played correctly, are said to "swing."

Most of the successful Swing Era bands followed a basic ensemble sound pioneered a few years earlier by Fletcher Henderson. Working in tandem with his gifted arranger, Don Redman, a musical prodigy who had graduated from college when he was 15 years old, Henderson adapted certain stylistic devices that became big-band conventions: riffs played in unison behind soloists, harmonized solo choruses, and brass and reed sections that shouted back and forth in call-and-response patterns. Later bandleaders relied on increasingly elaborate arrangements to make their bands sound distinctive, but they always stayed within the framework that Redman and Henderson had built. Benny Goodman, the most popular swing bandleader of all, even hired Henderson to write arrangements for his own orchestra.

Bursting out of Kansas City and on to the national scene, the Count Basie Orchestra represented a fresh approach to big-band jazz that helped enrich and extend the Swing Era. In contrast to other bands, Basie and his fellow musicians drove their group with pure, uncluttered swing provided by its incomparable rhythm section.

Each member of the section was a first-rate musician: Drummer Jo Jones, a former tap dancer, lightened the beat by accenting his cymbals rather than the bass drum, thereby making the beat driving but not heavy. Rhythm guitarist Freddie Greene strummed lines to keep the band steady and on course. "A performance has what I call a rhythm wave," he said, "and the rhythm guitar can help to keep that wave smooth and accurate." Walter Page, who had given the orchestra a rock-solid foundation since its earliest days in Kansas City, created bass sounds that served as the band's pulse.

Completing the rhythm section was Basie himself, whose percussive piano style helped make the rhythms sparkle. Basie favored his right hand and the upper part of the keyboard—practices that dated from sharing a piano with Bennie Moten and that he continued to follow because he wanted Page to be heard. "I've always enjoyed the bass," Basie explained. "We talk back and forth." Their conversations, in which Page played bass notes and Basie responded with treble notes, resulted in one complete sound, jointly created.

In the Basie orchestra's rhythm section, no one instrument was louder or more dominating than another. Playing together, they provided peerless support for the many fine brass and reed soloists in the band. "It was arguably the finest rhythmic foundation in jazz history," wrote jazz critic Gary Giddins, ". . . a security blanket and magic carpet."

Besides its esteemed rhythm section and gifted soloists, the Count Basie Orchestra was set apart by its expert use of the blues. Basing most of its arrangements on the instrumental blues form, the group revitalized big-band jazz by recalling the music's roots. One of the orchestra's most popular songs, in fact, was entitled "Swingin' the Blues," a perfect description of what the group did best.

When the smash 1938 engagement at the Famous Door thrust his orchestra into the limelight, Basie joined Duke Ellington as the country's best-known and most visible black bandleaders. Because most of the popular Swing Era bands were being led by whites—among them Tommy Dorsey, Artie Shaw, and Benny Goodman, the so-called King of Swing—Basie's rise to popularity also reminded people that jazz, founded on rhythm and blues, was a thoroughly black musical achievement. Based on the success of "One O'Clock Jump" and other rhythms that made dancers jump with joy, Basie for a time was even nicknamed the Jump King of Swing, which subtly challenged Goodman's reign.

To further remind the public of the contributions made by black musicians, John Hammond organized a show called "From Spirituals to Swing" at New York City's Carnegie Hall on December 23, 1938. The concert traced the development of swing, with each segment of the program showcasing a different black American entertainer and style of music, including blues sung by Big Bill Broonzy and gospel performed by Sister Rosetta Tharpe. The Count Basie Orchestra performed at various points in the show, in both small and large group combinations, and provided the evening's finale: several perfect examples of swing.

Marking the Carnegie Hall debut of the full Count Basie Orchestra, the concert was a complete sellout and a rousing success. Howard Taubman wrote in his review for the *New York Times*, "A good time was had by all—except, perhaps, by the manager of the hall, who might have been wondering whether the walls would come tumbling down." Hammond was especially pleased with the show. The evening's host could be seen bouncing in his seat in time to the lively music.

The Count Basie Orchestra enjoyed many similar successes as the 1940s began, and the group soon became a fixture of New York City's swing scene. The band appeared regularly at the Apollo and the Savoy in Harlem and at such midtown showcases as the Paramount Theatre, where it debuted in 1938, and the Strand, where it headlined in 1941. In 1943, it became the first black orchestra to perform at the Lincoln Hotel, where attendance at the shows set a house record, and at the Roxy Theatre, where in

1945, Basie and his musicians received $12,500 for a week of shows, one of the highest salaries paid to any group at that time.

The musicians also crisscrossed the United States, drawing the same enthusiastic responses wherever they performed. Following the band's 1941 engagement at Boston's fancy Ritz-Carlton Hotel, critics were unanimous in their acclaim: "There was no one in the place . . . who wasn't keeping time to the music," said one reviewer. Another observed, "The dancers rushed from the tables to the dance floor as if they were responding to an air raid warning."

Down south, the response was also positive. In 1940, more than 25,000 fans gathered for the orchestra's appearance at a dance in a North Carolina

The Count Basie Orchestra performs at New York City's Apollo Theater in 1940. "I wanted fifteen men to think and play the same way," Basie said of this newly enlarged band. "I wanted those four trumpets and three trombones to bite with real guts. BUT I wanted that bite to be just as tasty and subtle as if it were the three brass I used to use."

warehouse, which prompted the nervous promoters to call out the National Guard to help control the overflowing crowd. To accommodate the large number of fans, Basie agreed to play a second show. With that, the event proceeded without further disruption.

The band also went west. In the fall of 1939, Basie and his musicians made their first trip to California, for a series of shows that included an engagement at the San Francisco World's Fair. During the 1940s, the orchestra returned to the West Coast several times, heading often to Hollywood, where it appeared in such films as *Ol' Man*, *Hit Parade of 1943*, *Stage Door Canteen*, *Crazy House*, and *Reveille with Beverly* (one of vocalist Frank Sinatra's earliest films). A longtime movie fan, Basie was thrilled by his band's screen appearances because he got the chance to see how films were made and was able to meet such Hollywood personalities as Clark Gable and Bette Davis, two of his favorite stars.

By this point in their career, the band members were performing almost every day, traveling constantly, and taking little time off. Sometimes they played for a week or more in a single location, which gave the musicians a bit of a chance to relax. On other occasions, they were featured in a succession of one-night appearances separated by hundreds of miles, which caused the band members to spend countless hours on buses or trains as they shuttled off to their next performance. It was estimated that the orchestra sometimes covered more than 50,000 miles a year, and this in an age that saw very few people travel by air.

Basie and his musicians found ways to ease the monotony of such a grueling schedule. They gambled, played softball with other bands on the road, went out to eat, and shared talks and laughs. Some of them even grew fond of the seemingly endless stream of cities and bandstands; for them the road became a

way of life. In all cases, the band members got along famously with one another. "Even at our lowest ebb we all thought and felt as one man," said Jo Jones. "I was with the band fourteen years and not one single time did I see a fight."

In between their busy tours, Basie's orchestra continued to make records. In 1939, after the band had completed its agreement with Decca, Basie signed a new contract with Columbia Records, which released most of the group's songs for the next 10 years.

Some of the tracks the band recorded for Columbia, such as "Lester Leaps In" and "Dicky's Dream," were spontaneous group collaborations named for their featured soloists (in these cases, Lester Young and Dicky Wells, respectively). Other material came

No matter whether the band was performing before a live audience or recording an album, Basie observed everything his musicians did so he could keep the songs moving and the band playing together. Under his guidance, recalled Buck Clayton, "we became like a machine bent on nothing but swinging."

Basie guides his orchestra through a musical number for the 1943 film Stage Door Canteen. *A lifelong movie fan who learned to be a pianist by playing the musical accompaniment to silent movies, he was elated by the chance to appear on-screen—an opportunity he would receive many times.*

from a variety of sources. "Draftin' Blues" and "What's Your Number," for instance, were topical songs about conscripting men to serve in the armed forces during World War II, and "It's the Same Old South" was a sarcastic commentary about troubled race relations below the Mason-Dixon line. Recorded at the same 1940 session was "Stampede in G Minor" by Clinton P. Brewer, a prison inmate convicted of murdering his wife. No matter where the song came from, if the material was good, the band would record it.

During these years, a number of guest stars recorded with the band. Among them were tenor saxophonist Coleman Hawkins, who performed on "Feeding the Bean," and actor Paul Robeson, who sang "King Joe" at a memorable session in 1941. The lyrics had been penned by noted author Richard Wright, and at first Robeson had trouble with the song, a two-part blues about Joe Louis, the world champion boxer. Although Robeson was an accomplished vocalist, he had never sung the blues before. Coached by Jimmy Rushing, however, the actor successfully completed the recording. Afterward, Basie called working with Robeson "one of the great thrills of my life."

Appearing before capacity crowds and selling records steadily—in 1944 alone, the group sold 3 million records—the Count Basie Orchestra was consistently successful during most of the 1940s. For Basie personally, however, the decade was a period of transition. On October 30, 1941, his beloved mother died. Separated from her husband, Lilly Ann Basie had moved to New York and watched her son become a success. Bill, in turn, made sure that she lived comfortably. He even provided her with a car and chauffeur, making good on his childhood promise to get her an automobile.

Two years after her death, Basie suffered another loss when Fats Waller, his longtime friend and teacher, died of bronchial pneumonia. Along with James P. Johnson, Basie served as a pallbearer at Waller's funeral. He then performed at a memorial concert for Waller on April 2, 1944, at Carnegie Hall, where his music accompanied the dancing of another great Harlem performer, Bill ("Bojangles") Robinson.

Basie reached a happier milestone in 1942, when he married Catherine Morgan, a vaudeville dancer from Columbus, Ohio, whom he had met in Philadelphia years earlier while on tour with Bennie Moten. Because both he and Morgan were active in show business and traveled frequently, their paths had kept crossing, first in Kansas City and later in New York. Finally, after years of casual acquaintance, flirtation, and pursuit, Basie told Morgan, "If it's the last thing

I ever do, I'm going to have you as my wife." She accepted his proposal, and the two were married on Basie's birthday. "We spent a very unromantic honeymoon with Count's band on the road, doing one-nighters," Catherine Basie remembered, "[but] we had each other, and that was all that mattered."

On February 6, 1944, their first child, Diane, was born. In subsequent years, the Basies informally adopted three other children: two sons, Aaron Woodward III and Lamont Gilmore, and another daughter, Rosemarie Matthews. By 1946, the family was living in a comfortable home in St. Albans, New York.

Like his personal life, Basie's professional life in the 1940s was also marked by transition. With his orchestra continuing to tour and record regularly, its personnel kept shifting, for a variety of reasons. Some of the musicians, such as Walter Page, grew tired of the traveling. Others became anxious for new opportunities. And some, including Buck Clayton, Jo Jones, and Lester Young, had to leave the band during World War II because they had been drafted into the military. Several of the musicians who left the group would return to the band months or years later, only to leave again. Sometimes, after they had been replaced, their replacements would leave the band. By 1944, vacancies occurred so frequently that even Basie admitted, "It was pretty hard for me to keep track of all the changes in personnel in that band during that year."

Because of all these departures, the bandleader repeatedly faced the challenge of finding substi- tute musicians without risking the band's quality. Fortunately, he was an able judge of talent, and good musicians were eager to work with him. As the decade wore on, every section of his band included some of the era's premier players: Buddy Tate, Don Byas, Illinois Jacquet, and Lucky Thompson on tenor saxophone; J. J. Johnson and Vic Dickenson on

trombone; Al Killian, Clark Terry, and Joe Newman on trumpet; Earl Warren on alto sax; Helen Humes and Thelma Carpenter handling vocals; and numerous others.

As the membership changed frequently, Basie realized that the orchestra's dynamics had to change as well: The group could no longer be built on a foundation of familiar, reliable musicians working and improvising together. It was simply impossible, he knew, to keep on finding soloists who could improvise as brilliantly as Lester Young or Walter Page. Basie therefore sought to keep the orchestra sounding consistent by relying more heavily on arrangements written by band members (alto saxophonist Tab Smith, for one) or by hired arrangers

Author Richard Wright (left) and singer and actor Paul Robeson (center) were among the many notable figures who worked with Basie and his band. All three men combined their talents in 1941, when Robeson recorded "King Joe," a blues song written by Wright and performed by the Count Basie Orchestra.

Catherine Morgan was a vaudeville dancer who had met Basie when he toured the East Coast with the Bennie Moten Orchestra. They were married nearly a decade later, in 1942, and had four children, three of whom they adopted.

(such as Buster Harding). Basie himself would edit these arrangements, paring away everything he thought did not fit into the band's style or did not sound like Kansas City jazz. "He would cut out what he didn't like," Dicky Wells explained, ". . . until he got it swinging."

While Basie dealt calmly and successfully with changes in his band during the 1940s, the passage of time offered the greatest challenge to his leadership. During the first half of the decade, big bands fell victim to the harsh realities that World War II imposed on American life: Gas rationing restricted travel; entertainment taxes and curfews cut down attendance at concerts; and the military draft pulled many of the musicians off the bandstand and into the armed forces. By the time the war ended in 1945, the momentum of the Swing Era had been lost. Many bands had already broken up, and ballrooms and pavilions had closed their doors forever.

Just as significant, America's musical tastes had been changing. Early in the decade, the two types of music that had been featured by big bands—jazz vocals and instrumental jazz—began to polarize, until they split into two distinct camps. Vocalists, who had been minor attractions in most swing bands, became popular during the war years, singing about loneliness and parting—subjects with which many wartime listeners identified. Instrumental jazz had evolved as well. Saxophonist Charlie Parker, trumpeter Dizzy Gillespie, and a handful of other musicians popularized a new form of jazz known as bebop. Performed by small groups and characterized by unusual rhythmic improvisations, bebop made the big bands sound old-fashioned and soon caught on.

These economic and musical changes hammered away at the Basie band's fortunes. In 1947, the group began recording for RCA Victor, scoring hits with "Open the Door, Richard," a song inspired by a

Signaling the end of the big-band era, trumpeter John ("Dizzy") Gillespie was one of the musical pioneers who ushered in bebop, a revolutionary form of jazz, in the 1940s. Unfortunately for Basie, bebop made swing music sound out of date and prompted him to disband his large orchestra on January 8, 1950.

comedy routine, and "Did You See Jackie Robinson Hit That Ball?" which honored the first black major-league baseball player. Yet Basie spent most of the money he made from these hits on keeping the band together. According to trumpeter Harry Edison, the bandleader emptied his own bank account at least three different times so his musicians could be paid what he thought they deserved.

As a new decade approached, Basie realized his big band could not survive. The music scene had changed; there was not enough regular work to sustain a large jazz orchestra, and all the small groups were playing something new. His band had changed over the years as well: The only members left from the early days were Jimmy Rushing, Freddie Greene, and a few others.

On January 8, 1950, disheartened and nearly bankrupt, Basie decided to break up the band. "I just made up my mind," he said, "and then called everybody together and told them." Once filled with laughter and music, a golden era came to a sad and quiet end. ❧

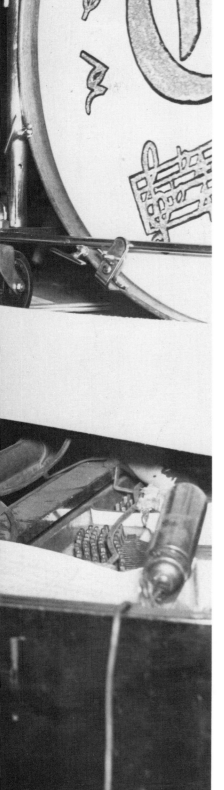

THE COMEBACK

IN THE WEEKS that followed the breakup of his big band, Count Basie organized and rehearsed a small group of six musicians. They debuted on February 10, 1950, in a six-week engagement at the Brass Rail, a Chicago nightclub. The sound of the sextet was leaner, more intimate than that of the Count Basie Orchestra, and for the next several months Basie continued to lead small ensembles comprised variously of six, seven, or eight members.

On the strength of Basie's reputation, his small groups were booked at such jazz clubs as the Hi-Hat in Boston and the Oasis in Los Angeles. They also made a few recordings. As a result, Basie was able to regain his financial footing and recoup some of the money he had lost at the end of the 1940s while trying to keep his large group together.

While he enjoyed modest success and a steady income, Basie was not altogether content. After a decade and a half of leading a big band, he did not feel satisfied accompanying just a few musicians. "In a small group . . . you have to play too much," he

After breaking up his orchestra in 1950, Basie spent most of the next two years touring and recording with small ensembles. He made occasional appearances with large groups during this period, however, which inspired him to lead a big band once more.

A member of the small ensembles Basie led in the early 1950s, saxophonist Marshall Royal became a central figure in Basie's second big band, which he began to assemble in 1952. Royal was appointed deputy leader of the group and quickly built the saxophone section into a premier unit.

joked. "I had to work too hard, and I had nothing to hide behind."

Occasional appearances at theaters such as the Apollo and the Strand further reminded Basie of the differences between leading a small group and a large one. For these bookings, workers' union rules obliged him to expand his group temporarily to a big-band size. With more than a dozen instruments playing once again in unison, these makeshift orchestras stirred in Basie a deep nostalgia. "There's nothing like the sound of those big sections," he said, recalling his former band's depth and power.

Such experiences convinced Basie that he was happiest when leading a big band. He knew that the jazz and popular music scenes had changed since his initial success, but his instincts told him to ignore the risks and follow his heart. "We need you out here with a big band again," singer Billy Eckstine told him. Other contemporaries offered him similar words of encouragement and support, until Basie made up his mind to build a new orchestra.

He knew, however, that it could not be like his former band—a closely knit team of improvisers—because he had found it impossible to keep the same musicians together for extended periods of time. But he believed that a large group of talented players, working with arrangements that kept them sounding fresh and consistent, could still generate enough precision, drive, and swing to thrill listeners.

In the spring of 1952, Basie and Marshall Royal, a versatile musician who had emerged as Basie's deputy, started to assemble such a group in New York. As soon as enough suitable musicians were found, they went into rehearsal and performed at one-night-only bookings to help them grow comfortable playing together. "We cut up a lot of the old [band's] arrangements," Royal said in describing the group's rebuilding process. "We changed some tempos, played others as is and took arrangements from just about everybody." By summer the big band was ready for a Manhattan showcase.

The second Count Basie Orchestra makes its debut at New York City's Birdland in 1952. Except for guitarist Freddie Greene, the band featured an entirely new lineup of musicians.

Basie (fifth from right) and his wife, Catherine (fourth from right), pose with members of the Count Basie Orchestra for a group portrait in 1954. The band was in the midst of its first tour of Europe.

On July 24, 1952, the orchestra debuted at Birdland, a nightclub located around the corner from Swing Street, at Broadway and 52nd Street, and named after one of bebop's reigning kings, Charlie ("Bird") Parker. Audiences greeted Basie and the reborn group with warmth and enthusiasm, pleased to discover that they were not trying to imitate Basie's old band but instead performed music that was familiar in style but also fresh and alive. Reviewing the engagement, the jazz magazine *Down Beat* said, "Basie has managed to assemble an ensemble that can thrill both the listener who remembers 1938 and the youngster who has never before heard a big band like this."

Typically, Basie's comments after his new group's debut were much more modest. "Somehow," he said,

"I knew that it was going to be even better after we worked together for a longer while." When it came to assessing his orchestra's performance, the band-leader was, as usual, correct.

As the group toured and recorded in the months following its debut, Basie saw the lineup continue to change, adding new musicians who further refined the big band's precision and skill. Along with Royal, who played alto saxophone and other instruments while serving as musical director, the Count Basie Orchestra during the 1950s included such talented musicians as drummer Sonny Payne, bassist Charlie Fowlkes, trombonist Al Grey, and trumpeter Thad Jones. The tenor saxophonists—always featured musicians in a Basie band—included Eddie ("Lockjaw") Davis, Frank Foster, and Frank Wess (who also played jazz flute, a new and unusual addition to the big-band sound). Guitarist Freddie Greene, the sole veteran of the All-American Rhythm Section, rejoined the band in 1950 and never left, thus becoming the musician who played with Basie the longest.

Although Basie's lineup continued to be impressive, listeners could hear that the orchestra's collective sound was different from that of Basie's original big band. Unlike the earlier group, whose style was rooted in jam sessions and improvisation, the sound of Basie's big band of the 1950s was born on paper, created by different arrangers. Also, Basie no longer relied on individual instrumentalists, whom he knew could leave the band at any time. Instead, he used arrangements that emphasized the sound of the entire orchestra.

Basie's arrangers thus became the new band's featured personalities. Some of them, such as Frank Foster and Thad Jones, were members of the orchestra; others, among them Neal Hefti and Johnny Mandel, were not. Whatever their status, they all wrote specifically for Basie, composing original arrangements or adapting standards that utilized the band's talents while maintaining a steady swing. Their scores enabled the different instruments and sections of Basie's band to function like colors on a painter's palette: Some stood alone and others were combined, all to create a spectrum of moods and textures.

More than ever before, Basie believed that sturdy arrangements would keep his band sounding consistent and reliable, even as its personnel shifted. He also believed that a regular flow of new arrangements would help the group absorb changes in the music world, thereby keeping its sound fresh and contemporary. When asked how his band stayed up-to-date following the rise of bebop, Basie replied teasingly that his arrangers just "put mink coats on the chords."

Despite their fresh faces and new arrangements, Basie's big band of the 1950s established its popularity through live performances, just as his first orchestra had done. Although the big-band era had ended years earlier and bebop had turned jazz from dance music into listening music, Basie discovered that the public had not forgotten him. His rejuvenated band was able to find bookings all over the country. In New York, for instance, it began to appear regularly at Birdland three to four months out of every year and always during the Christmas season.

The group was greeted by enthusiastic, appreciative audiences outside the United States as well. In March 1954, the orchestra made its first trip to Europe, performing in Denmark, Germany, Holland, Belgium, France, and Switzerland. Wherever his big band appeared, Basie delighted audiences with his piano playing, his handful of notes that provided witty and vibrant contrast to the driving brass and reed sections. The orchestra's success on the road confirmed that there were still many listeners interested in hearing big-band music and that Basie-style

Music impresario Norman Granz produced several records with the Count Basie Orchestra from 1952 to 1957. Able to break down racial barriers in the United States by sponsoring concerts with integrated seating, he said that "jazz is an ideal medium for bringing about a better understanding among all peoples."

swing, in particular, had an undeniably persistent appeal.

In addition to concert appearances, records helped spread the new band's popularity. Shortly after it was organized, the group began recording for Clef and Verve, two labels founded by Norman Granz, an ardent promoter of jazz, its musicians, and their rights. Of the numerous fine recordings the group made for Granz, two memorable instrumentals earned permanent places in Basie's repertoire: "Shiny Stockings," a medium-tempo ballad written and arranged by Frank Foster, used coolly muted trumpets sparring against tough brass for an icily romantic effect. Conversely, the bold, strutting "April in Paris," arranged by jazz organist Wild Bill Davis, showcased the group's tight precision. Twice at the end of this song the music halts and Basie's voice can be heard. "One more time!" he says, and later, "One more, once!" Each time, the band obeys him and plays another rousing chorus. Listeners loved the novelty of the song's false endings, and the record became an enormous hit.

As Basie's new group became established through concerts and recordings, fans and critics began referring to it as his New Testament band (after the second part of the Christian Bible, to distinguish it from his original, Old Testament band). To commemorate Basie's long tenure as a bandleader, John Hammond, Willard Alexander, and Alan Morrison of *Ebony* magazine arranged a tribute for him at New York City's Waldorf-Astoria Hotel on Halloween night, 1954, the 28th anniversary of his first band's departure from Kansas City. More than 400 notable guests, including Benny Goodman and singers Lena Horne and Nat ("King") Cole, attended the gala and spoke in his honor. No speech pleased Basie more than the one given by his father, who told the crowd, "This is my son, whom I am well pleased with."

Late in the evening, the curtains in the dining room parted and revealed two bands: One comprised of Basie's former sidemen, including Jimmy Rushing, Buck Clayton, and Lester Young, who had reunited for the occasion; the other was Basie's current orchestra. The bandleader performed a few numbers with each group, and the contrast was obvious: His first band swung with spirit and personality, like an old reliable steam train, whereas his new band soared like a powerful jet, sleek and polished. The link between the two was, of course, the quiet man at the piano who drove them both with a series of subtle signals—a pointed finger, a nod of his head, a wink, or a smile.

It was clear that despite their differences, both bands were extensions of their leader's personality. The Count Basie Orchestra might have changed over the years, but it always had Basie as a common denominator. Because of him, whenever the alumni of his first big band made guest appearances with the new group, as they often did in subsequent years,

Vocalist Joe Williams joined the Count Basie Orchestra on Christmas Day, 1954, and quickly helped the band reach the top of the popular music charts. A commanding singer, Williams scored hits with his versions of "The Comeback" and "Every Day I Have the Blues."

they played comfortably alongside whomever was in the orchestra.

Two years after Basie's reborn band began to achieve recognition and success, the addition of vocalist Joe Williams improved the already special chemistry of the New Testament group. A former brush salesman, Williams had sung briefly with Basie's sextet in Chicago in 1950. Now, four years later, on Christmas Day, he became a full-fledged member of the band. Williams's big, strong voice rang with clarity and could easily be heard over Basie's blaring brass section. A versatile singer, he was a master of the blues and could perform other types of songs just as well.

On May 17, 1955, Williams recorded "Every Day I Have the Blues" with the Count Basie Orchestra, and it became their breakthrough record. Written by bluesman Memphis Slim, the track lasted for more than five minutes—far longer than most songs then being cut—and was issued on both sides of a 78 RPM (revolutions per minute) disc. Despite its unusual

Two of the jazz world's greatest bandleaders, Basie and Duke Ellington (right) collaborate in a music studio in 1961. The recording session marked the first time the two pianists had worked together on an album.

length, the rollicking song became an immediate success and even proved popular with fans of rhythm and blues and rock and roll, two up-tempo styles of music then gaining in popularity. (At the same session, the orchestra cut another track, "The Comeback," whose title seemed to sum up Basie's newfound success.)

Williams's performance of "Every Day I Have the Blues" was outstanding; his voice seemed to jump from the record, demanding to be noticed. The record made it apparent that just as Basie had been able to incorporate changes in jazz into his band's music, so had he found in Joe Williams a singer who made the orchestra sound completely up-to-date, in step with popular music as well as with jazz. Williams ultimately performed with Basie's orchestra for 17 years and received equal billing on the records they made together. And there never was any competition between the two men, because each man had helped the other reach a larger audience. Basie, in fact, referred to Williams as "my number one son."

By 1957, Basie's orchestra was more successful than it ever had been. That June, he and his musicians shared a stage with jazz vocalist Sarah Vaughan and thus became the first black band to headline at the Waldorf-Astoria. The engagement was so successful that they were held over for six weeks and were invited back for another set of appearances later in the year.

Basie's orchestra also made two tours of England in 1957. During the musician's first trip, which marked the band's British debut, Princess Margaret, the sister of Queen Elizabeth, saw it play twice in one day, which prompted a local newspaper to run the headline ROYALTY SALUTES BASIE BAND. On a return visit later in the year, the orchestra met and played for the queen at a royal command performance, the first American band to be accorded such an honor. To commemorate the occasion of jazz royalty greeting British royalty and Count meeting queen, Basie and his orchestra recorded "H.R.H.," a song dedicated to Her Royal Highness.

In 1957, Basie also signed a contract with Roulette Records, a company for which he and the band recorded more than 20 albums. Their debut release on the label, a collection of Neal Hefti arrangements, was particularly special. Simply titled *Basie*, with a cover photograph of an atomic blast, the record was in part a response by the bandleader to some critics who had complained that his simple piano style had become clichéd and that he could no longer play like he once did.

Beginning with the opening track, "The Kid from Red Bank," and continuing through the album, Basie made his presence felt, unleashing a series of dazzling keyboard runs that were like snapshots of his past, containing echoes of New York City stride and Kansas City jam sessions, that his orchestra complemented perfectly through brisk, contemporary arrangements. The record, upon release, was widely thought to be a masterpiece—a coherent, consistent example of modern big-band swing. At midcareer, Basie had silenced his critics and proved that at age 53 he was more in control than ever.

In 1960, Basie celebrated his silver anniversary—25 years as a bandleader. Now regarded as one of America's most esteemed musicians, he performed with his orchestra at the inauguration of President John F. Kennedy in 1961 and four years later at the inauguration of President Lyndon B. Johnson. Basie also continued to make concert appearances around the globe and to produce popular records, aided largely by a talented young musician-arranger named Quincy Jones. Basie had met Jones years earlier, at the Palomar Theater in Seattle, after the latter had managed to sneak backstage by carrying an empty instrument case under his arm. Reminded perhaps of his own youthful ambition, the bandleader agreed to try out some of Jones's arrangements and was pleased with the result.

As Jones grew older and more musically experienced, his friendship and collaborations with Basie continued. By 1963, four of the albums he had

Basie rehearses with Ella Fitzgerald (left) and Frank Sinatra (right) for a show at New York City's Uris Theatre in 1975. In addition to appearing with the two popular vocalists, Basie also recorded albums with each singer.

arranged for Basie's orchestra were on the pop charts at the same time. That same year, Jones's arrangement of the song "I Can't Stop Loving You," which Basie had recorded, won each of them their first Grammy Award, for Best Dance Performance and for Best Instrumental Arrangement. Jones, who has since gone on to many other accomplishments, including making his own hit records and producing best-selling albums by singer Michael Jackson, still credits Basie with helping him get his start. "He was my uncle, my mentor, my friend," Jones acknowledged, "the dearest man in the world."

While continuing to lead his band in the 1960s, Basie decided to make use of his stature as a leading public figure by lending his support to the growing civil rights movement. The usually quiet bandleader, who had often witnessed racial discrimination during his long tenure as a traveling entertainer, began to speak out against prejudice and call for equality among all races. He publicly endorsed sit-ins, the organized protests against racial segregation that began to spread through the South in 1960, and in December 1963 he joined the students at Florida State University who picketed an off-campus restaurant that refused to serve black customers. During the decade, Basie and his wife, Catherine, also worked for such progressive organizations as the National Urban League, the National Conference of Christians and Jews, and the United Negro College Fund in an effort to foster social change.

As American society went through turbulent times in the 1960s, its popular music changed, too. Rock and soul music dominated the attention of young listeners, and jazz, which was becoming more specialized, lost a large portion of its audience. Accordingly, Basie tried to broaden his appeal, with mixed results. Although he made fine jazz albums during these years—the 1960 *Kansas City Suite* arranged by Benny Carter, for instance, and a collaboration with Duke Ellington in 1961—Basie and his orchestra also recorded insipid collections of pop material, songs by the Beatles, and themes from James Bond films, none of which adapted well to swing and thus squandered the musicians' considerable talents.

To sustain some measure of integrity and success, Basie and his orchestra made recordings with such great American popular singers as Ella Fitzgerald, Tony Bennett, and Sammy Davis, Jr. Their collaborations marked some of the band's finest work during the 1960s. Basie's most notable association at this time, however, was with Frank Sinatra, whose talent and popularity seem to withstand any changes in popular music. The orchestra's musicians, with their impeccable timing and precision, were the perfect accompanists for Sinatra, who knows how to swing a vocal. Their combination proved potent: Together they made several top-selling albums (for Sinatra's label, Reprise) and toured successfully. About his chance to work with Basie, Sinatra, who first rose to prominence during the big-band era, said, "I've waited twenty years for this moment."

Besides keeping Basie active and successful during the 1960s, his work with Sinatra earned them both tiny roles in one of the era's major historical events. On July 20, 1969, U.S. astronauts Neil Armstrong and Buzz Aldrin became the first men to land on the moon. Just before they left their spacecraft to walk on the rocky lunar surface, Aldrin switched on a tape player he had brought with him. Into airless space boomed the song "Fly Me to the Moon," arranged by Quincy Jones, sung by Frank Sinatra, and performed by Count Basie and His Orchestra. Having his song chosen as the first music to be played on the moon, Bill Basie from Red Bank, New Jersey, had indeed come a long way. ◀◆▶

9

"THE SAME OLD BEEF STEW"

BY THE 1970s, Count Basie was no longer just a beloved entertainer. After more than three decades in the music business, he had become a jazz institution. Still, he did not slow down. Year after year, he and his orchestra maintained their rigorous schedule of performing live and making records.

In 1971, the group traveled to the Far East, appearing in Hong Kong, Burma (present-day Myanmar), Laos, Thailand, and Singapore for the first time. Basie and his musicians also journeyed to New Zealand and Australia, where in Perth they played before an opening night crowd of 10,000. It was estimated that their constant touring and recording, along with their appearances on television and in films such as *Blazing Saddles*, earned them more than half a million dollars per year, a large sum of money for that time.

Even though Basie's reputation kept growing, the orchestra's music changed very little. Dozens of musicians had passed through the band since Basie reestablished it in 1952, but the sound remained fixed, thanks to the library of arrangements they used.

Basie performs at the University of Missouri at Kansas City after receiving an honorary degree from the conservatory of music. A high school dropout, he said that the occasion marked "one of the happiest days of my life."

Their repertoire, greatest hits drawn from every era of the Basie band, was widely known to musicians and audiences alike. The Basie style was so familiar, in fact, that young musicians who joined the orchestra hardly needed to rehearse because they had been hearing the music virtually all their life. When someone asked Basie, "What's the band going to play tonight?" he would reply, "The same old beef stew."

The band's combination of blues and swing may have offered few surprises, but it remained hearty, for Basie always made sure that his group sounded rhythmically alive. Despite his advancing age, he remained an expert bandleader, his abilities honed by decades of experience. If some of his musicians came to a performance drunk, for example, Basie would be sure to choose a song that featured them, putting the musicians on the spot and making sure they learned their lesson.

Offstage, Basie remained a simple man; worldwide success did not change his habits. For relaxation he enjoyed betting on horses; watching baseball games and rooting for the New York Yankees; playing the organ; and collecting electric trains, a hobby that recalled his life on the road—and perhaps his band's driving sound. Each Christmas, his wife would give him a new item for his train set, which he had installed in the basement of their New York home. His only personal flourish was a yachting cap, which he wore constantly and became his trademark.

In the mid-1970s, after living in New York for more than 25 years, Basie and his family moved permanently to Freeport in the Bahamas, settling in a residence with tall columns and walls of pink marble. He called the structure his family's "house of happiness" but joked that he was on the road so much that he was never able to enjoy his new home's luxury. "My family lives down in the Bahamas," he would say. "I live in the Greyhound Bus."

In many ways, the road *was* his true home. He toured up to 49 weeks a year with the orchestra, and he seemed to gain vitality from the young musicians who joined his band and kept it swinging. "There are nights that give all musicians wonder," he said, "and you keep hoping for another night of wonder."

Basie also found renewed vigor in recording. In 1973, Norman Granz started a new jazz label, Pablo (after the artist Pablo Picasso), and began to record Basie in a variety of musical settings: with large and small groups, in concert, and in the studio. The different combinations seemed to stimulate Basie and yielded fresh and surprising results. Among his favorite sessions for the label were those he did with Canadian pianist Oscar Peterson in 1974. Peterson's elaborate technique contrasted sharply with Basie's, which was simple and efficient, and the two musicians alternated piano runs like a game of tag. In honor of their friendly sparring and compatibility, the resulting album was titled *Satch and Josh*, after two baseball players who starred in the Negro leagues: pitcher Satchel Paige and catcher Josh Gibson.

As Basie entered his seventies, he gave no indication of retiring. But in 1976, age began to take its toll. On Labor Day weekend, he suffered a heart attack and was ordered to rest for six months. Following his recuperation, he returned to his orchestra as if nothing had happened, determined and eager to continue. "Once you hit your seventies," he said, "you can't really expect to feel in tip-top condition every day anyway. So you just hang on in there, and you go out to make the gig, and you feel much better doing that than you do just lying around worrying about yourself." One sideman put it another way: "He's too used to the road to quit now."

Not surprisingly, the road, and Basie's success, brought him back many times through Kansas City, where his bandleading career had begun. In Septem-

Basie signs his autograph for two young fans. "I've been able to do what I enjoy doing and make a pretty good living," he wrote in his autobiography, Good Morning Blues, *"and also make a name for myself and a reputation that stands for something."*

Managing to keep his orchestra active—despite changes in popular music and in the band's lineup—until his death in 1984, Basie saw the group become famous not only for its talent but for its durability. Today the Count Basie Orchestra continues to perform—and thus carries on its founder's legacy.

ber 1977, the city staged a special weekend celebration to honor him. Feted by the townspeople and given special concerts, he received an honorary degree from the conservatory of music at the University of Missouri at Kansas City. The former dropout called the event "one of the happiest days of my life." Two years later, on his 75th birthday, Basie returned to Kansas City to appear at the city's new Uptown Theater and also to give a free concert in a small park near Twelfth and Vine streets, where half a century earlier he had looked for work.

By 1980, Basie had developed arthritis and could no longer walk without assistance. Typically, he refused to let his deteriorating health dampen his spirit or restrict his activity. To get to his piano onstage, he drove a motorized scooter with a small horn that he would toot playfully at the audience. "The point will come when the road tours stop," he admitted, "but I won't be ready for it. Somebody else will make that decision; my wife, the doctor, the bookers, the people—or the Almighty."

Catherine Basie, who had begun to accompany her ailing husband on the road, passed away in April 1983. Basie's own health continued to deteriorate in the year following her death, although he kept on performing and also managed to conclude the first draft of his autobiography, *Good Morning Blues*, written in collaboration with music historian Albert Murray. Finally, on April 26, 1984, four months short of his 80th birthday, William Basie died of cancer.

His funeral was held a few days later at the Abyssinian Baptist Church in Harlem, not far from the places where he had first mastered his piano-playing technique. As the church filled to capacity, thousands more gathered outside in the rain to pay their respects, while many of Basie's musicians assembled to bid their leader one last good-bye. Joe Williams's voice trembled as he sang "Come Sunday," a spiritual composed by Duke Ellington, to the mourners inside the church. Aaron Woodward III, one of Basie's adopted sons, delivered the eulogy, in which he spoke of his father's band and said that Basie "would not want you to forget for one minute that they were the best on planet Earth."

After the service, Freddie Greene, Basie's friend for almost 50 years, seemed to speak for all the musicians. "I am standing here," he said, "and I don't know what to do now that he's gone."

As it turned out, he and the others did precisely what Basie, the most durable of performers, would have preferred: They kept the band intact. In the years since his death, the Count Basie Orchestra has continued to give concerts throughout the world, led first by Thad Jones and now under the direction of Frank Foster.

Basie, of course, was always willing to share the spotlight. The secret to swing, he had learned, was the joy of cooperation. In a career that spanned the course of jazz history, from his early years as a Harlem pianist to his apprenticeship as a Kansas City sideman and his decades as a bandleader, he had observed it was through teamwork that a musician found perfect rhythms—and success. ❧

APPENDIX: SELECTED DISCOGRAPHY

Count Basie's music has been captured on dozens of recordings, most of which are still available. The following sampling includes albums from the different stages in his career and should serve as a good introduction to his work.

BASIE WITH THE BENNIE MOTEN ORCHESTRA

Basie Beginnings (RCA/Bluebird)

THE FIRST COUNT BASIE ORCHESTRA

Best of Count Basie (MCA)
The Essential Count Basie (Columbia)
From Spirituals to Swing (Vanguard)
Good Morning Blues (MCA)
One O'Clock Jump (Decca/MCA)
Super Chief (Columbia)

THE COUNT BASIE ORCHESTRA'S COMEBACK

April in Paris (Verve)
Basie (also known as *The Atomic Mr. Basie*) (Roulette)
Basie in London (Verve)
Basie Plays Hefti (Roulette)
Chairman of the Board (Roulette)
Sixteen Men Swinging (Verve)

THE COUNT BASIE ORCHESTRA IN ACCOMPANIMENT

with Tony Bennett:
Basie Swings, Bennett Sings (Verve)

with Ella Fitzgerald:
Ella and Basie (Verve)

THE COUNT BASIE ORCHESTRA IN ACCOMPANIMENT (*cont.*)

with Frank Sinatra:
Sinatra-Basie   (Reprise)
It Might as Well Be Swing   (Reprise)
In Concert: Sinatra at the Sands   (Reprise)

with Joe Williams:
Count Basie Swings . . . Joe Williams Sings (Verve)
The Greatest—Count Basie Plays/Joe Williams Sings Standards   (Verve)
Sing Along with Basie

THE COUNT BASIE ORCHESTRA: THE 1960s AND BEYOND

Count Basie Jam   (Pablo)
First Time: Count Meets the Duke   (Columbia)
Kansas City Suite   (Roulette)
Li'l Ol' Groovemaker . . . Basie   (Verve)
Montreux '77   (Pablo)
Oscar Peterson and Count Basie: Satch and Josh   (Pablo)

CHRONOLOGY

———— ❧ ————

1904   Born William Basie on August 21 in Red Bank, New Jersey

ca. 1919   Learns how to play the piano

1924   Moves to New York City; tours the United States with Katie Krippen and Her Kiddies, a vaudeville act in the *Hippity Hop* revue

1925   Returns to New York City; befriends stride pianists James P. Johnson and Thomas ("Fats") Waller

1926   Tours the black vaudeville circuit with Gonzelle White and Her Band

1927   Arrives in Kansas City; becomes hospitalized for four months with spinal meningitis

1928   Begins to call himself Count; joins the Blue Devils band and tours the Southwest

1929   Returns to Kansas City; joins the Bennie Moten Orchestra; cuts first record, "Rumba Negro"

1933   Becomes bandleader of Count Basie and His Cherry Blossom Orchestra

1935   Rejoins the Bennie Moten Orchestra; forms Count Basie and His Barons of Rhythm and is discovered by John Hammond

1936   Signs with a management agency; the Count Basie Orchestra makes its New York City debut

1937   Basie begins to record for Decca Records; cuts "One O'Clock Jump"; Billie Holiday joins the Count Basie Orchestra

1938   Basie begins smash engagement at New York City's Famous Door; performs in "From Spirituals to Swing" at New York City's Carnegie Hall

1939   Begins to record for Columbia Records

1942   Marries Catherine Morgan

1943   Makes first appearances in Hollywood films

1944   Daughter, Diane, is born

1950   Basie disbands the Count Basie Orchestra; begins to tour and record with small ensembles

1952	Re-forms the Count Basie Orchestra
1954	Makes first tour of Europe; Joe Williams joins the Count Basie Orchestra; Basie receives tribute from his peers at New York City's Waldorf-Astoria Hotel
1955	Cuts breakthrough record, "Every Day I Have the Blues"
1957	Makes first and second tours of England and gives a royal command performance; begins to record for Roulette Records
1963	Wins first Grammy Award
1969	Basie's recording of "Fly Me to the Moon" becomes first song to be played on the moon
1971	Basie tours Far East for the first time
1973	Begins to record for Pablo Records
1976	Suffers a heart attack
1977	Receives an honorary degree from the University of Missouri at Kansas City
1984	Concludes first draft of autobiography, *Good Morning Blues*; dies of cancer on April 26

FURTHER READING

Basie, Count, and Albert Murray. *Good Morning Blues*. New York: Fine, 1985.

Clayton, Buck, with Nancy Miller Elliott. *Buck Clayton's Jazz World*. New York: Oxford University Press, 1987.

Dance, Stanley. *The World of Count Basie*. New York: Da Capo Press, 1980.

Gourse, Leslie. *Every Day: The Story of Joe Williams*. New York: Da Capo Press, 1985.

Hammond, John, with Irving Townsend. *John Hammond on Record*. New York: Penguin Books, 1977.

Horricks, Raymond. *Count Basie and His Orchestra*. Westport, CT: Greenwood Press, 1972.

Kliment, Bud. *Billie Holiday*. New York: Chelsea House, 1990.

———. *Ella Fitzgerald*. New York: Chelsea House, 1988.

Morgun, Alun. *Count Basie*. New York: Hippocrene Books, 1984.

Murray, Albert. *Stomping the Blues*. New York: Vintage Books, 1982.

Ostransky, Leroy. *Jazz City*. Englewood Cliffs, NJ: Prentice-Hall, 1978.

Pearson, Nathan W., Jr. *Goin' to Kansas City*. Urbana: University of Illinois Press, 1987.

Russell, Ross. *Jazz Style in Kansas City and the Southwest*. Berkeley: University of California Press, 1982.

Sheridan, Chris. *Count Basie: A Bio-Discography*. Westport, CT: Greenwood Press, 1986.

Wells, Dicky, with Stanley Dance. *The Night People*. Boston: Crescendo, 1971.

INDEX

PICTURE CREDITS

Basie Estate: pp. 20, 21, 96, 101, 118; From the Collection of the New Jersey Historical Society, Newark, NJ: pp. 24, 25; Frank Driggs Collection: pp. 2–3, 10–11, 13, 15, 18–19, 23, 28, 30, 33, 37, 48, 50–51, 54, 59, 62–63, 66–67, 69, 70, 72, 75, 78, 82, 84, 89, 91, 95, 98–99, 100, 102, 107, 108, 111; Courtesy of the Kansas City Museum, Kansas City, MO: pp. 40–41, 42, 43, 45, 47, 53, 97; The Music Division, The New York Public Library, Astor, Lenox & Tilden Foundations: pp. 3, 22, 34, 56, 105; University Archives, University of Missouri–Kansas City: pp. 114–15, 117; Ken Whitten, Las Vegas: p. 92

BUD KLIMENT lives in New York City and works for the Pulitzer Prize Board at Columbia University. He specializes in film and music writing and has contributed to the *Village Voice, Video,* and other periodicals; his writing has also appeared in *The Book of Rock Lists, The New Trouser Press Record Guide,* and *The Virgin Guide to New York.* He is the author of *Ella Fitzgerald* and *Billie Holiday* in Chelsea House's BLACK AMERICANS OF ACHIEVEMENT series. Both titles were named as Best Books for the Teen Age by the New York Public Library.

NATHAN IRVIN HUGGINS, one of America's leading scholars in the field of black studies, helped select the titles for the BLACK AMERICANS OF ACHIEVEMENT series, for which he also served as senior consulting editor. He was the W.E.B. Du Bois Professor of History and of Afro-American Studies at Harvard University and the director of the W.E.B. Du Bois Institute for Afro-American Research at Harvard. He received his doctorate from Harvard in 1962 and returned there as a professor in 1980 after teaching at Columbia University, the University of Massachusetts, Lake Forest College, and the California State University, Long Beach. He was the author of four books and dozens of articles, including *Black Odyssey: The Afro-American Ordeal in Slavery, The Harlem Renaissance,* and *Slave and Citizen: The Life of Frederick Douglass,* and was associated with the Children's Television Workshop, National Public Radio, the Boston Athenaeum, the Museum of Afro-American History, the Howard Thurman Educational Trust, and Upward Bound. Professor Huggins died in 1989, at the age of 62, in Cambridge, Massachusetts.